Lost Landmarks of Mississippi

HITE HOUSE

Lost Landmarks of Mississippi

MARY CAROL MILLER

University Press of Mississippi / *Jackson*

Publication of this book was made possible in part by Mr. and Mrs. E. B. Robinson, Jr.

www.upress.state.ms.us

Frontis: White House Hotel, courtesy of James S. Love, III; above: Wesson Hotel, courtesy of Mississippi Department of Archives and History.

Designed by Todd Lape

Printed in Canada

10 09 08 07 06 05 04 03 02   4 3 2 1

Library of Congress Cataloging-in-Publication Data

Miller, Mary Carol.
Lost landmarks of Mississippi / Mary Carol Miller.
p. cm.
ISBN 1-57806-475-9 (cloth : alk. paper)
1. Architecture—Mississippi. 2. Lost architecture—Mississippi. I. Title.

NA730.M7 M55 2002
720'.9778'09034—dc21   2002001736

British Library Cataloging-in-Publication Data available

Contents

Acknowledgments

This book is possible only because of the dedication and generosity of countless people in towns and cities across Mississippi who care enough about their communities to document their history and share it with others. Without their unselfish donations of time and talent, many of the state's "lost landmarks" would be forgotten forever. In a more official capacity, the staff at the Mississippi Department of Archives and History provides invaluable expertise and access to photographs, architectural descriptions, and preservation documents. Special thanks are due Richard Cawthon and Todd Sanders of MDAH. Richard first suggested *Lost Landmarks* as a follow-up to *Lost Mansions of Mississippi* and provided a list of likely inclusions. Todd has located rare photos and answered dozens of questions, and I am grateful for both his and Richard's encouragement and support.

Chapter 1: Hubert McAlexander, Chesley Thorne Smith, Leigh McWhite, Buzzy McGuire, Rosemary Williams, Kristy White, Callie Young, Donna Dye, Jack Garner, Rachel Pyron, Mary Dean Hollis, Mary E. Jeffries, Howard M. Evans, Jr., Debra McIntosh, Tommy Covington, William Washburn

Chapter 2: Pat Mowry, Kat Bergeron, Gordon Cotton, Jerry McWilliams, Jim Lacey, Belinda Roark, Martin Hegwood, Mary Ann Fontaine, Joan Gandy, Thomas Gandy, Mimi Miller, James S. Love, Dee Joyce, David Wiseheart

Chapter 3: Patricia Young, Milton Winter, Jolee Hussey, Ann Gerache, Bea Gotthelf, Mark Greenberg, Sara Criss, Hank Lamb

Chapter 4: Dannie Weatherby, Elizabeth Lewis, Annie Ruth Brown, Sarah Hallum, Tommy Hallum

Introduction

Mississippi's architectural legacy, in its most recognizable form, is one of white mansions with soaring columns and Corinthian capitals, the enduring symbols of the Cotton Kingdom that flourished briefly in the nineteenth century. Stanton Hall, Waverley, Riverview, Walter Place, and dozens of other homes stand today as tangible proof that Mississippi once was a land of phenomenal prosperity and architectural styling.

The early Mississippians who built those mansions were largely transplanted pioneers from the old Atlantic Coast states. As their original log cabins and clapboard dogtrot houses gave way to Greek Revival plantation manors and Gothic townhouses, they yearned for the finer elements of society that they had left behind in Virginia, the Carolinas, and Georgia. Tiny frontier towns like Columbus and Aberdeen and Port Gibson needed courthouses, churches, schools, and colleges. Increasingly secure in the prosperity that soaring cotton prices brought, Mississippians turned their attention from providing themselves with shelter to building the landmark structures that would complement their memorable houses. That emphasis on architectural excellence would be manifested even through war and Reconstruction and into the next century, when cotton was no longer king and Mississippi struggled to catch up with the rest of the nation.

In the 1800s, the first unified effort of a community often brought forth a school. Holly Springs and Corinth were little more than crossroads with a few homes and stores when their citizens banded together to fund academies like the University of Holly Springs, Holly Springs Female Institute, and Corona Female College. Several tiny towns ambitiously vied for the honor of hosting the new University of Mississippi. Oxford claimed the prize, but a host of other communities boasted their own "institute" or "college," and many of these campuses were the sites of remarkably elegant buildings. The Civil War led to the closing of most of the institutions and the physical loss of a regrettably large number of the structures, but the postwar era saw a resurgence in academic building, including schools for freed slaves and true college-level ventures.

The influx of new settlers to Mississippi in the 1820s and 1830s brought a wave of religious emphasis that had been absent in the territorial days. Churches were a vital element of the towns which grew up in the Indian cession lands. Most started in a parishioner's home and were eventually replaced by a wooden chapel. As fortunes grew and congregations expanded, ecclesiastical landmarks appeared, their architectural exuberance reflecting devotion to God and an abundance of spare cash. Greek Revival masterpieces like First Baptist Church of Columbus were reminiscent of the old-line churches of Savannah and Charleston. Gothic chapels dotted the state, ranging from the simplicity of Christ Church in Church Hill and St. John's on Lake Washington to the grandeur of St. Peter's in Oxford. An increase in Jewish migration in the mid-1800s culminated in the building of fine synagogues and temples in Natchez, Vicksburg, Port Gibson, and other towns.

As new counties were carved from Indian lands, each one required a seat of government. Simple log courthouses set down on green space designated as "the square" were soon surrounded by stores, law offices, and lodges. They were then replaced by more elaborate buildings, fronted with columned classical facades and topped with clock towers and cupolas.

Beyond the needs of individual communities, the state as a whole was demanding architectural symbols of its success. Jackson grew from a mosquito-infested backwater to a thriving city boasting William Nichols's classical statehouse and Governor's Mansion and the forbiddingly gothic State Penitentiary. Even the State Insane Asylum was designed to highlight Mississippi's prosperity and opulence. In Oxford, Nichols laid out a university that would still be considered one of America's most attractive a century and a half later.

Mississippi remained an agricultural state from its origin until well into the twentieth century. True industrial architecture of the type that defined New England and mill states such as Georgia and the Carolinas was never a priority. This was not due to any lack of creativity but merely indicated the unwillingness of the state's entrepreneurs to invest in the manufacturing stages of cotton production. A few cotton mills and clothing manufacturers would grow to epic proportions, but practically the only true industrial structures to be built before World War I were the massive lumber operations that thrived for a thirty-year period in the Piney Woods region.

Hospitality was the only "industry" that gained a foothold in the antebellum era. Sprawling resort hotels lined the Gulf Coast, attracting winter-weary northerners and rich Louisianans and Alabamians eager to escape New Orleans and Mobile. Mississippians favored the spas and resorts scattered throughout the state, flocking to take the "healing" waters and relax on the verandas of Cooper's Well, Artesian Springs, and Castalian Springs. A later wave of hotel expansion brought huge hotel complexes to Biloxi, Gulfport, and Pass Christian, as railroads and then highways made travel to the Magnolia State easier.

Like their domestic counterparts, the ranks of Mississippi's landmark buildings have been decimated by time and neglect. Many of the earliest were lost during the Civil War, their very spaciousness and visibility dooming them to impressment as hospitals and headquarters for rival factions. Courthouses and college buildings were easy targets for vengeful or careless soldiers, and numerous towns had lost their most notable public landmark by the end of that war.

Time itself has been another enemy of the state's early architecture. Styles change, a community's needs shift, and a proud courthouse is razed to make way for more modern structures. Lightning strikes, old wiring sparks, or a faulty chimney sends flames into dry, rotted wood, and a church or dormitory or hotel is reduced to rubble. Tourists find the beaches of Florida more desirable than the muddy waters of the Mississippi Sound, and great hotels go dark and are doomed to the wrecker's ball.

Scattered throughout the state, deep beneath layers of parking lot asphalt or hidden in weed-choked lots, are the remnants of Mississippi's lost landmarks. Old photographs capture them in their days of glory, and yellowed newspaper clippings describe opening celebrations, proud dedications and, inevitably, demise and demolition or loss through fire or storms. Most have totally vanished, leaving no trace that they ever occupied their sites. Others, like Artesian Springs, still stand but are so far gone that all hope of reclamation is lost. Only rarely, as with the White House Hotel in Biloxi, are they pulled back from the brink of extinction and given new life. That landmark will soon reopen, brought back to its original splendor by the same family that saw it through its best days half a century ago. Perhaps it will serve as an example for future preservation of Mississippi's remaining landmark buildings.

Lost Landmarks of Mississippi

Chapter One

Schools and Colleges

DURING ITS FIRST HUNDRED YEARS OF STATEHOOD, Mississippi was home to a plethora of private colleges, institutes, seminaries, and academies. The state's commitment to public education was shaky at best, more often completely absent, and realistically nonexistent until Reconstruction. To offer their children some rudimentary means of acquiring knowledge, individuals and communities poured their personal resources into private schools. Some of these institutions never progressed beyond a crude grammar school level, while others claimed a true college-level standard, providing the sons and daughters of planters and businessmen with a balanced and useful education. The smallest may have been nothing more than a handful of students meeting in a teacher's home. The most prosperous and ambitious academies erected impressive Greek Revival buildings and provided boarding for dozens or even hundreds of young people. Almost all of these schools have totally vanished, victims of war, economic downturns, and the rise of public education.

Mississippi's educational history is a roller coaster of high hopes and lofty expectations, often followed by broken promises and dashed dreams. Governor W. C. C. Claiborne arrived in Natchez in 1802, brimming with the educational ideals set forth by Thomas Jefferson and the Northwest Ordinance. That 1787 document embraced the principle that "schools and the means of education shall forever be encouraged" on America's frontiers. Mississippi was very much a frontier, just four years beyond Spanish rule, when Governor Claiborne urged the legislature to establish a "seminary of learning."[1] In a scenario which would recur discouragingly often over the years, that body covered itself by giving lip service to education but failing to back it up finan-

Lowrey Dormitory, Blue Mountain College *(See page 27.)*

cially. Jefferson College was brought forth with much fanfare and self-congratulation and thirty-four distinguished trustees appointed to guide its fortunes. Funding for the state's first school was a bothersome detail that the legislature brushed aside. Jefferson College existed only on paper until 1811, when a preparatory department opened in the hamlet of Washington. After various land deals and a lottery failed to provide enough money to expand the offerings, the 1816 legislature "loaned" the trustees six thousand dollars, allowing them to finally pull together a college-level department.

As Jefferson College tottered along, Mississippi's seventy-five thousand citizens welcomed statehood in 1817. They were scattered throughout a scant one-third of the new state's land area, living mainly along the Mississippi River and the lands south of present-day Jackson. That isolation, coupled with the already-creeping sectionalism which would retard progress in so many areas, kept education firmly on the low rung of the priority ladder. Nine "academies" of questionable pedigree had received state charters by the early 1820s, including Franklin Academy in Jefferson County and Madison Academy in Claiborne County. Wealthy planters sent their children north to college or arranged for private tutors. For those unable to attend an academy or hire a teacher, education simply didn't exist.

The abysmal lack of educational offerings could not be blamed on Mississippi's early governors. George Poindexter surveyed the available schools in 1820 and pushed hard for a tax-supported "Literary Fund." Appalled at the quality of Jefferson College and the tiny academies, he observed, "There is scarcely a seminary of learning among us worthy of the name; perhaps not one . . . Jefferson College, which has been so richly endowed by the general government, and on which our liberality has been so freely bestowed, is comparatively an empty dome with pensioned preceptors."[2]

Governor Poindexter was right about the "empty dome." Jefferson College regressed to prep school status just after its first three-story brick building was completed. A 6 percent tax intended to fund county schools squeaked through the legislature, but it proved so unpopular that it was repealed in 1823. The citizens of Columbus were the exception in managing to open and maintain a decent public school, Franklin Academy. The rest of the state shrugged its collective shoulders at the outrageous notion of education for the masses.

The charter of hapless Jefferson College was revoked altogether in 1826. The school would reemerge as a military prep school three years later, and it struggled through repeated closures for another century. Undeterred by its failure, a few visionaries put their financial support behind various academies and institutes which were struggling to keep their doors open. Most closed before one term was even finished, but two schools overcame the obstacles to survival. Hampstead Academy, in Clinton, was the most noteworthy and enduring of these small schools. With broad local support and a legitimate academic pedigree, it vied for recognition as the official state university. A name change to Mississippi Academy furthered that ambition. The legislature went so far as to transfer some of the funds from Jefferson College to the institution which would become Mississippi College, but never sanctioned it as a state school. Jeremiah Chamberlain's Oakland College, in Lorman, was practically the only other reasonable option for higher education in the early 1830s.

Despite the lack of a coherent educational system, Mississippi was a magnet for emigrants in that decade and the one that followed. Millions of acres of cheap land in the north and central sections of the state were opened for development after removal of the Choctaw and Chickasaw tribes. Settlers from the Carolinas, Virginia, and Georgia poured in, founding new towns that sprang up from the forests like mushrooms. These new Mississippians found their academic options severely limited. There was no legislative support for a public school system and, with the exception of Mississippi Academy and Oakland College, no in-state institutions of higher education.

One governor after another hammered away at the legislature, demanding a plan. The "Literary Fund" had grown to fifty thousand dollars, and pressure was building on the lawmakers to establish a state university or designate one of the existing private schools to fill that need. Governor John A. Quitman felt that building a university was premature. With no broad network of grammar and preparatory schools, a true college would have ill-prepared students. "The means of a plain, practical education should be extended to every free child in the county, cost what it may . . . I recommend to the legislature the adoption of, as early as possible, an effective common school system . . . Until the establishment of a general system of common school education, it would be but vain ostentation in the State to build up seminaries in their instruction in the higher branches of learning."[3]

Even casual visitors to Mississippi were disturbed by the lackadaisical attitude toward formal education. J. H. Ingraham toured plantations and towns throughout the state in the mid-1830s, and was not impressed. "The education of young children on plantations is much neglected . . . Two-thirds of the planters' children of this state are educated out of it . . . Their own institutions are neglected and soon fall into decay."[4]

The newcomers who had pulled up stakes in established states grew impatient with Mississippi's glacial progress, and often took matters into their own hands. Before lots were even laid out in Holly Springs, a group of landowners had pledged eight thousand dollars to build the University of Holly Springs. These backers petitioned the legislature for a formal charter to grant college degrees. Miraculously, their petition was granted, and the state's first university opened its doors in 1837. Financial reverses closed the school within a few months, but the momentum was building to create a decent public college for a population that had almost tripled in ten years.

To fill the gap left by legislative inertia, "liberal arts colleges" were opening at the rate of several per year. Once again, Holly Springs led the way with its backing of the Holly Springs Female Institute. It began in "a modest but comfortable structure of hewn logs with clapboard roof, overhung by friendly oaks."[5] By 1838, the cornerstone had been laid for a massive two-story Greek Revival school serving 140 students, 60 of them boarders. Academic standards were high. A. M. Clayton noted that "its educational advantages, were, from the earliest day, of a high order."[6] Graduates were awarded the "Mistress of Polite Literature."

Holly Springs wasn't the only town that grew impatient with the state's educational outlook. By 1840, there were almost four hundred locally sponsored "common" schools, enrolling more than 8,000 pupils. Seventy-one "academies" claimed 2,480 students, and eight "colleges" taught 545 more. Governor Alexander McNutt recognized this trend and followed the gubernatorial tradition of pushing for a statewide system of public schools. "The State is bound by the highest obligations of duty and patriotism, to educate all her children . . . The Legislature that establishes a system of free schools . . . will be immortalized in the annals of the State."[7]

The legislature continued to ignore the cries for a public school system. Sister states were building prestigious universities, and Mississippi had to have one, too, despite the fact that its population had tragically limited access to preparatory schools. A committee studied potential sites and chose Oxford over Mississippi City by one vote. The University of Mississippi was formally chartered in 1844. New governor Albert G. Brown pounded away on the need for "a well-regulated system of free schools"[8] to feed the university, but as usual the legislature acted halfheartedly. A weak and ultimately useless Common School Act, passed in 1846, was whittled down until it was stripped of all effectiveness. In later years, Edward Mayes would wryly note that "the educational movement of that period is a curious study."[9]

In a state where most of the children remained illiterate or minimally trained, the plans for a grandiose university continued. William Nichols, architect for the state capitol and the Governor's Mansion, designed the first buildings and the grounds of the university campus. A classical main building, two faculty houses, two dormitories, and a steward's hall rimmed a tree-shaded "circle" in the midst of 640 acres. The Lyceum cornerstone was laid in July 1846. Its carpenters and craftsmen received their first pay in gold, delivered to Oxford personally by the board of trustees' treasurer after a horseback ride up the Natchez Trace from Jackson.

The long-awaited University of Mississippi opened in the fall of 1848. Students and professors slogged through mud and construction debris to occupy their unfinished accommodations. Each faculty house served two teachers and their families. The dormitories housed seventy-two young men. Within just a few years, their numbers had grown and the need for "a large commodious hall for assemblies and commencement" was evident. The chapel went up as the final building on William Nichols's circle.

As the state university developed, it faced competition from privately funded institutions throughout the state. In keeping with the rhetoric of the day, these were designated "seminaries," "halls," "institutes," and "colleges." Individuals, particularly clergymen, were often the driving force behind these schools. A few stock companies formed by local citizens financed others. Recognizing the distances that separated many of their students from the facilities, most offered boarding. Clientele was usually limited to "male" or "female," although a few were coeducational or paired with a nearby school for the opposite sex. Curriculums ranged from the most elemental basics to a few true college-level offerings.

The physical plants of these schools were as varied as their academic credentials. Some never progressed beyond the parlor of a professor's home. Others, with more of an economic base, invested heavily in noteworthy buildings. William Nichols moved on to Lexington when his work at the university was complete and, in the last years of his life, designed and built the striking temple-form Lexington Male and Female Academy. In Pontotoc, the Presbyterian church took control of the Pontotoc Female College and moved it into a massive columned Greek Revival structure in 1853, renaming it Chickasaw College. Grenada's Baptist Yalobusha Female Institute moved from the old Union Hotel into a four-story, fifty-thousand-dollar building. Mississippi Academy, rejected as the state university, had nevertheless prospered under Baptist

Chickasaw College, ca. 1900. Photo courtesy of Mississippi Department of Archives and History (MDAH).

control. The chapel built there in 1860 remains one of the state's most enduring and impressive Greek Revival monuments.

Oddly enough, given the secondary status of women in antebellum society, some of the most impressive educational structures of the time were built on the campuses of female colleges. Corinth's Corona College, Holly Springs Female Institute, Chickasaw College, and Calhoun Institute were all housed in expensive, elaborate buildings. Central Female Institute, sister school to Mississippi College, was centered around Institute Hall and was adding a huge secondary building when the Civil War stopped its construction.

After sixty years of procrastination, Mississippi was inching toward a semblance of academic legitimacy, at least for the favored few who could afford the university or one of the better academies. The Civil War brought that progress to an abrupt halt. Four years of conflict wrecked the state's emerging educational network financially and physically. Eighty percent of the men at the University of Mississippi signed up with the Confederate service when war broke out in the spring of 1861. Only four students appeared for the fall term. The faculty resigned, and the college was closed for the duration. Chancellor Frederick A. P. Barnard, commenting on the deserted campus before his return to the North, said, "We are indeed inhabitants of a solitude. . . . Our University has ceased to have visible existence."[10] Dr. A. J. Quinche was appointed the keeper of the campus buildings. He moved into the observatory and briefly opened a primary school for thirty boys.

Only a few schools remained open during the war. Some lost their entire faculties to the military; others went bankrupt as the Confederate economy crumbled. Their buildings, usually the largest available in a community, were often requisitioned for hospital service. Governor J. J. Pettus authorized the conversion of the university's academic and dormitory space to hospital wards when war moved closer to north Mississippi. Every building on campus was utilized after the Battle of Shiloh, with two thousand wounded men squeezed into space adequate for only a thousand. A forest of tents popped up on the grassy circle to handle the overflow. Those who didn't survive were taken to the tiny Magnetic Observatory, ever after known as the "Dead House." At least seven hundred soldiers are buried on the campus.

The university was abandoned by Confederate forces and subsequently occupied by Union troops. Remarkably little damage was done to the college buildings, a situation which some attribute to the friendship between Chancellor Barnard and General Sherman or to the influence of geology professor Eugene Hilgard. The most unfortunate incident involved a foray into the Lyceum by Kansas Jayhawkers in search of alcohol. Finding and consuming it, they then rode their mounts into Barnard Observatory. Burton Harrison's sister was in the observatory at the time:

> I shall never forget our horror when we looked out of the little upstairs window in the observatory that P.M. and saw a lot of wild devils (excuse the expression, no other word expresses them) come galloping from the Campus way, with long blue army overcoats flying behind them, tall peaked caps on their heads, and each one flourishing at arm's length a bright, new, tin coffee pot, stolen from some store in Oxford. They bore down upon the Observatory, burst in the main doors, and spread themselves all over the building, breaking up apparatus and chemicals, and then rushing into the dwelling apartments, frightening us women nearly to death. Fortunately, however, they had not gone very far in their course, when some officers arrived on the spot, and fairly clubbed them into obedience to their orders to get back to camp . . . Just then they spied a large demijohn of Antimony wine, and each fellow declaring that it was whiskey, immediately filled his coffee pot, and drank enough of the stuff to make him deadly sick and virtually crazy.[11]

The university was spared when General A. J. Smith torched Oxford. Other colleges were not so fortunate. Corona Female College, the pride of Corinth, was used first as a Confederate hospital, then a Federal one, as northeast Mississippi fell to occupying forces. As the troops evacuated in 1864, they set fire to the main building of the college. An eyewitness recalled the sight seventy years later, remembering "the great piles of hot bricks. A man . . . said people were going to use the bricks to help rebuild the town. Corona College was no more."[12] A similar fate was in store for the 1838 Holly Springs Female Institute building. Both armies had used it as an infectious disease ward as Holly Springs changed hands sixty-two times. In the last withdrawal by Federal troops, it was set ablaze. Whether this was a precautionary measure necessitated by its contamination or a senseless act of war is unknown.

Macon's Calhoun Institute served a drastically different role in the Civil War. Mississippi's government was on the run after the fall of Vicksburg, fleeing to Meridian, Enterprise, Columbus, and finally Macon. The legislature took over Calhoun Institute, with the house meeting in the main building's salon and the senate relegated to the "Red House" on the grounds. Governor Charles Clark was in Macon when the war ended. He commented on the conclusion of four years' destruction: "All the pomp and circumstance of battle had passed away, and this Andalusia of the western hemisphere, in a few brief years, had become a wreck of its former self . . ."[13]

This "wreck of its former self," as Clark so aptly described Mississippi, had to be rebuilt from the ground up. Among myriad other problems, the educational system was decimated. The university struggled to resume its duties, but most of the old "academies" and "institutes" were gone for good. Others reorganized and limped along, including Grenada, Lexington Female, Hillman, and Chickasaw colleges. They were joined by a wave of church-sponsored schools for the newly freed slaves. The American Missionary Association founded Tougaloo College in 1869. The Freedman's Aid Society used the state's first independent black church, Holly Springs's Asbury Methodist congregation, to organize Shaw University the same year. Recognizing the nearly universal illiteracy rate among freedmen, Shaw admitted all ages, from children to adults.

Mississippi's lawmakers had treated public education as an unwanted stepchild for decades. It took a Reconstruction legislature to finally devise a system that mandated real schools statewide, available to all children, black and white. Despite grumblings about waste and taxation, the government decreed that each county and each city with more than five thousand citizens would be a school district, with those schools open at least four months of the year. On this inauspicous basis, Mississippi's public school system became a reality at last. By 1878, sixty-four thousand white children and seventy-one thousand black children were enrolled in school. Those numbers reflected barely a third of the population which was eligible for public schools, but it was nevertheless a giant leap forward from antebellum days.

Before southern Democrats regained control of state government, the "carpetbaggers" and "scalawags" made one other lasting contribution to higher education. Oakland College in Lorman had struggled for years following the violent 1851 death of founder Jeremiah Chamberlain in a dispute over slavery. The state purchased the campus to serve as America's first black land grant college, Alcorn Agricultural and Mechanical. A white land grant university, Mississippi A & M, would follow at Starkville.

The last two decades of the nineteenth century saw a rebirth of private colleges, more enduring and legitimate than their antebellum predecessors. Confederate General M. P. Lowrey bought land a few miles south of Ripley and named his 1873 college for the "blue mountain" on which it would be built. His family controlled the school for ninety years, even after the Baptist Convention bought the campus.

The American Baptist Home Mission Society started Natchez Seminary for black students in the old Marine Hospital. In 1883, the institution bought fifty-two rolling acres on the northern limits of Jackson and moved to the capital city, taking the name of Jackson College. Founders Hall was built there in 1885. Five years later, Methodist-sponsored Millsaps College opened next door to Jackson College and offered to buy the black school out. The trustees of the small school resisted until 1902, when they signed over the deed to the land and Founders Hall, moving their own operation to Lynch Street. Millsaps would flourish in the location, and the relocated Jackson College would expand to become Jackson State University.

Half the cost of founding Millsaps was borne by Major Reuben Webster Millsaps, a wealthy Jacksonian. His son-in-law, Louis Fitzhugh, left Whitworth College in Brookhaven and bought the palatial home of Colonel Jones Hamilton on Boyd Street, just a few blocks from the state capitol. The house, known as Belhaven, sheltered Fitzhugh's school for young ladies. In 1895, the house and two adjoining buildings were destroyed in a fire; the college reopened just two weeks later in downtown Jackson. Fitzhugh rebuilt on Boyd Street, and the school grew steadily on that campus until its buildings were once again destroyed by fire in 1910. The Presbyterian Church took over the charter and built a brand-new campus in the fashionable north Jackson subdivision which would come to carry the college's name.

The arrival of the twentieth century found Mississippi's public school system an accepted fact, despite its deficiencies and a chronic lack of funding, severe for white schools and disgraceful for black schools. This transition to a taxpayer-funded, widely available network of local schools all but eliminated the private preparatory schools which had dominated academia during the previous century. One of the last private boarding schools to open was Mississippi Heights Academy in Blue Mountain. Dr. B. G. Lowrey, son of Blue Mountain College's founder, was president of the girls' school in the early 1900s. He formed a stock company to purchase land on the commanding hill just east of campus and built a towered school at the crest of its summit. Sixty boys enrolled for the initial semester in 1904. Ten years later, Mississippi Heights was sold outright to Professor J. B. Brown, who ran it as his personal domain for thirty years. He took local boys, boarders, and troubled youth referred from Memphis and throughout north Mississippi, often educating them from childhood through the college years. When bad health forced his retirement during World War II, the school dwindled and disappeared.

"Prof" Brown's Mississippi Heights was the last, outdated vestige of a system which had struggled to provide some form of enlightenment and education, no matter how rudimentary, to generations of Mississippi students. Nothing remains of the school except the tower bell, bolted to a memorial stone on the Tippah County hill where Prof Brown labored for four decades to improve the lives of his pupils. That monument is unusual, for most of Mississippi's educational landmarks have vanished without a trace, even the memory of their alumni erased with the passage of time. Corona College and Hillman College are nothing but chunks of concrete foundation hidden beneath grassy fields; Holly Springs Female Institute and Calhoun Institute are shadows around the public high schools which now stand on their sites. These and other lost schools served their purpose and disappeared with Mississippi's belated realization that all of its children deserved an education.

Holly Springs Female Institute

Holly Springs was an 1830s boom town, a village growing from a tavern stop in the woods to a place with a population of several thousand within a matter of months. Cheap Indian lands lured settlers from the East Coast and Tennessee, eager to bring their established values and culture into this untouched territory.

Holly Springs Female Institute, ca. 1860. Photo courtesy of Chesley Thorne Smith.

Five months before the first official town lots were sold, a group of Holly Springs residents gathered to plan a school for their daughters. A teacher was hired and "a modest but comfortable structure of hewn logs with clapboard roof, overhung by friendly oaks"[14] was built on Hernando Road. The Holly Springs Female Institute was a reality.

Early records are scarce, but the school must have been welcomed. Within two years, the trustees were laying the cornerstone for an ambitious project, a Greek Revival classroom/dormitory structure rising two stories above a raised basement. Principal Consider Parish opened the 1839 session in the new building and shepherded his charges toward their goal, the degree of "Mistress of Polite Literature." Subjects offered in 1840 included English grammar, U.S. history, Grecian and Roman antiquities, chemistry, and epistolary composition. One hundred and forty girls could be accommodated in classes, with sixty of those living in-house as boarders. They came from all over Mississippi and neighboring states.

Holly Springs Female Institute was overseen by a succession of headmasters trained at Princeton and Yale. It prospered throughout the 1850s in spite of competition from nearby Franklin Female College. Local boys went to Chalmers Institute or St. Thomas Hall, and Hodding Carter has noted that "[b]y 1850, Marshall County was spending more on higher education that the rest of the state put together, excluding the budget for the University of Mississippi."[15]

The Female Institute's future might have been limitless but for the advent of the Civil War. In 1862, as General Grant's armies marched across north Mississippi, the school was closed in preparation for its use as a hospital. Holly Springs physician Dr. Charles Bonner was directed by the state to set up an infectious disease ward in the rooms recently used for elocution, chemistry, and the study of Grecian antiquities.

The war spared few corners of Mississippi, but Holly Springs took a particularly repetitive beating. The town changed hands more than sixty times and suffered devastating raids by both armies. Wounded and dying soldiers filled the halls of the Female Institute for two years. As Federal troops evacuated Holly Springs in 1864, the building burned. It remains unclear whether this was a wanton act of destruction, an attempt to dispose of a contaminated hospital, or simply an accident.

Several of Holly Springs's private schools reopened following the war, but the Female Institute was gone forever. Its site was taken for the town's first public school and is now the location of Holly Springs High School.

Early Buildings of the University of Mississippi

In June 1846, University of Mississippi trustee Thomas Williams loaded fifteen thousand dollars in gold into two saddlebags and began an arduous and dangerous journey up the Natchez Trace from Jackson to Oxford. The small fortune he was carrying was the first payment for William Nichols's carpenters and bricklayers laboring on the landmark building which would come to be known as the Lyceum.

Nichols had turned from his triumphant career in Jackson to his new job as the architect for Mississippi's flagship university. His original plan called for a ring of classically inspired academic and residential structures surrounding a forested circle. The Lyceum would be the centerpiece, flanked on either side by a men's dormitory and a faculty house. Behind the Lyceum was the functional Steward's Hall, plainer and more utilitarian than the "circle" structures.

Each of the men's dormitories was divided into three sections; the southwest dorm's divisions were dubbed Franklin, Madison, and Washington, while the northwest dorm's were Jefferson, Lafayette, and Rittenhouse. Each dorm held thirty-six students. Further out on the circle, the two faculty residences were three-story structures divided down the middle to accommodate two families each. Since the university hired only four professors, including the president, this was ample housing for the staff.

University of Mississippi Men's Dormitory, ca. 1860. Photo courtesy of University of Mississippi Special Collections.

When the students arrived on campus in the fall of 1848, their dorms were not quite finished and the campus itself was an ongoing construction site, littered with debris and building materials. Nevertheless, classes did get under way, and within three years the trustees were discussing the need for a third dorm. That building completed Nichols's circle, but it served as a chapel and meeting place rather than a dormitory.

In the late 1850s, Chancellor F. A. P. Barnard's observatory was under construction, and the school's reputation in the field of science was growing. The U.S. Coastal Geologic Survey invited Mississippi to participate in their experiments, provided they could supply a building free of magnetic interference to house the necessary instruments. A small structure was built close to the observatory, unique in its use of wooden nails and lead-lined bricks over a dirt floor. It may have been called the "Dead House" from its creation, due to the lack of magnetic interference, but it probably acquired that name when it took on a more ominous role.

Chancellor Barnard returned from a visit to the Smithsonian in April 1861 to find the campus in an uproar:

> On my return I was told that the flag of Mississippi had been flying on one of the dormitories during my absence and on the opposite dormitory a band of loyal students had kept the flag of the United States flying for ten days. At the same time I found that a large portion of

University of Mississippi Faculty House (L) and Chapel (R), ca. 1860. Photo courtesy of University of Mississippi Special Collections.

> the students had formed themselves into a military company called 'The University Grays,' and had demanded of the governor, John J. Pettus, to be mustered into the Confederate service . . . The whole population seemed, in fact, to have suddenly gone wild, and I considered it my duty to remain silent, but the trustees of the college met at a session held in May, immediately after the attack on Fort Sumter, and I presented them with my resignation . . . [The board] persuaded me to withhold my resignation at least til the opening of the fall session, at which time they expressed the utmost confidence that we would be able to resume operations with our full numbers. They insisted on the extreme improbability of a serious war, and I think that the general opinion of the people was that a peace of some kind would be patched up during the summer.[16]

The trustees couldn't have been more mistaken. Only four students showed up in the fall of 1861. Barnard lamented, "We are indeed inhabitants of a solitude . . . Our

University of Mississippi South Dormitory, ca. 1900. Photo courtesy of MDAH.

University had ceased to have visible existence."[17] The college was shuttered, and Chancellor Barnard left for New York. Within a few months, the war was on Oxford's doorstep. Governor Pettus authorized the establishment of a military hospital in the campus buildings. After Shiloh, the dorms, faculty houses, observatory, and Lyceum were overflowing with dead and dying soldiers. The Dead House lived up to its name, serving as a morgue. As Oxford passed from Confederate control to Union occupation and back to southern oversight, the college's graveyard filled with seven hundred soldiers.

Miraculously, the university escaped the destruction unleashed on Oxford. Damage to the campus buildings was minimal, and the school reopened after peace was established. During the remainder of the nineteenth century, the original buildings were maintained to some degree and new ones added. The old Steward's Hall was used for a variety of purposes, including faculty housing. One professor, Dr. Hedleston, lived there so long that it came to be known as Hedleston House. The original dorms were in a sad state by 1908, when a state inspection noted that "[t]here existed upon the

University of Mississippi Steward's Hall, ca. 1860. Photo courtesy of University of Mississippi Special Collections.

campus but two dormitories, and those were old, and entirely inadequate to house comfortably the students."[18] The northwest dorm was the first to be demolished, followed by the southwest dorm in 1919. The bricks from that building were used to build tenant houses on a Delta plantation.

The Steward's Hall hung on until 1930, when it was demolished to allow a walkway from the Lyceum to the new Johnson Commons. Ironically, the tiny Dead House was the only one of the earliest campus buildings, other than the Lyceum, the observatory, and the chapel, to survive late into the twentieth century. It served as faculty housing, as a clandestine meeting place for the DKE fraternity during the period of Greek banishment, and as a site for Chi Omega pledge inititiations. The law journal converted it into offices during the 1940s, but it was finally dismantled to make way for law school expansion in 1958. The Lyceum and chapel, the last survivors of William Nichols's original work, have been renovated and serve as vital elements of the modern university, along with the still-vibrant observatory.

Calhoun Institute, ca. 1860. Photo courtesy of MDAH.

Calhoun Institute

One of the most architecturally notable buildings that was used for education in antebellum Mississippi is remembered chiefly for its brief role in state government and war rather than its contributions to academia. Calhoun Institute was built in Macon by Professor W. R. Poindexter sometime around 1856. In the few years of its existence before the Civil War, it achieved a reputation as an excellent girls' school, probably operating on a college preparatory level.

The main structure of Calhoun Institute was a three-story frame block with a square cupola crowning the flat roof. Porticoes on the front and rear facades were each supported by full-height Doric columns, and Gothic-style chimneys lined the edges of the roof. The only existing drawing shows elaborately landscaped grounds and sweeping drives.

Calhoun Institute's claim to fame lies in its role as the home of the Mississippi legislature during the 1864 and 1865 sessions. After the Union occupation and destruction of Jackson in 1863, the state government took on a nomadic cast. The governor and other state officials, carrying what records and official items they could, fled first to Meridian, then Enterprise, Columbus, and finally Macon. Governor Charles Clark was inaugurated in Columbus but spent most of his war-shortened administration in Macon. Major Charles W. Allen loaned his mansion out for the governor's residence, and the representatives who could make their way across ravaged Mississippi gathered in the main salon of Calhoun Institute. The senate met in a building on the institute grounds known as the Red House.

War's end found Mississippi's makeshift capital still at Macon. Governor Clark's young daughter, Annie, recorded the scene at the "Governor's Mansion" when the telegram arrived: "Pa handed Ma a telegram to read. I could see by their faces that something dreadful had happened and I ran to the porch where the telegram was being handed around for all the family to read. Yes, it was all over. General Lee had surrendered at Appomattox! Like a thunderbolt it fell upon us . . . I remember feeling astonishment that we were not all dead."[19]

For the Clark family, the worst was yet to come. Annie's father was imprisoned at Fort Pulaski for a short time on charges of treason. The remnants of the government moved back to Jackson, abandoning Calhoun Institute. The school remained largely unused for thirty years and was demolished around 1900. The public high school occupies the site today.

Corona Female College

At the junction where the Memphis and Charleston Railroad met the Mobile and Ohio Railroad, just a few miles into Mississippi from Alabama and Tennessee, the town of Corinth quickly grew from a crossroads into a major trade center. In 1857, its fifteen hundred citizens lined up behind Reverend L. B. Gaston, a North Carolinian recently relocated from Oxford. Reverend Gaston planned to open one of America's first legitimate women's colleges, and his fellow Corinthians pledged forty thousand dollars for its construction.

Corona Female College was fully accredited by the state and opened preparatory and college-level departments in July 1857. Within a year, ninety young women were enrolled, traveling from Mississippi, Tennessee, Alabama, and Texas for their educa-

Corona Female College, ca. 1862. Photo courtesy of Northeast Mississippi Museum, Corinth.

tion. They were housed and taught in one huge building, designed and built by the Swiss master craftsman Martin Siegrist. Three stories of dark brick with tall pedimented windows and towering brick columns with Ionic capitals, Corona was an impressive sight in the small town. Its silver dome was visible for miles.

Corinth's railroads were an asset in the antebellum era, but their very existence put the town and college in peril during the Civil War. As armies gathered in nearby Shiloh, Reverend and Mrs. Gaston sent their students home, but refused themselves to evacuate. They would soon be engulfed in a nightmarish hell. Mrs. Gaston remembered the spring of 1862: "The sound of guns first reached us Sunday morning; we hurried from the breakfast table to the yard and listened to the continued roar. 'Twas like the far away sea waves when they break upon the shore. The sick from the hospitals were being sent away to make room for the wounded who would certainly be brought from Shiloh. A few days and the battle was over, the Confederates claiming the victory, the Federals sullenly giving back, neither side able to continue the contest. During the four weeks following the battle, the town was filled with sick and badly wounded men."[20]

Corona College was commandeered as the primary Union hospital. The nine-year-old daughter of one of the Federal surgeons lived with her father in the converted school. Her memories of the building were vivid many years later: "It was a large three-story structure of brick, with a portico in front supported by massive pillars . . . To me it was the Castle Beautiful."[21] The Gastons stayed on, hosting northern doctors and nurses with grace and hoping to reopen their college when war ended.

When Union forces evacuated Corinth in January 1864, several buildings were torched, including Corona Female College. W. E. Small described the scene: "I was born in 1860 . . . only a little fellow when Corona College burned but I remember it very distinctly. The Federal soldiers were leaving Corinth. All day long they had been marching by our house . . . Many of them would call out to me as they passed and some would come nearer and pat my cheek . . . That night our house was awakened because of the fire at Corona College. I remember going to a window and watching the flames. The next morning I was taken over to the scene of the fire and remember the great piles of hot bricks. A man came along and asked to borrow my toy wagon I had with me. He said people were going to use the bricks to help rebuild the town."[22]

Corona College, which stood for less than seven years altogether, and only four of those as a school, was never rebuilt. Its site has been taken over by commercial development, with only a few sections of the foundations to be found beneath the dirt.

Grenada College

The city of Grenada grew out of a peaceful compromise between two competing towns, Pittsboro and Tullahoma, which merged into one community on July 4, 1836. The resulting town spanning the Yalobusha River grew rapidly and followed the lead of its neighbors in promoting higher education. Several schools opened under the sponsorship of various churches. In 1850, the Methodists founded Bascomb Academy, followed the next year by the Baptists with Yalobusha Female Instititute. Though it went under a variety of names over the years, the Baptist school would be the most enduring.

Classes for Yalobusha Female Institute were first held in Grenada's Union Hotel. Within a few years, enough money was generated to build an imposing Greek Revival main building, with a columned portico above a raised basement. One and a half mil-

Grenada College, ca. 1900. Photo courtesy of MDAH.

lion bricks were used for the impressive exterior and the four-and-a-half-foot-thick interior walls. Fifty-two "apartments" housed one hundred boarders and classes for several hundred day students.

The Civil War brought an end to the first life of the school. The students were sent home and the buildings used as hospitals following the Battle of Shiloh. After the war, the school reopened briefly as the Emma Mercer Institute before a group of Grenada citizens bought it and changed the name to Grenada Female College. The deed was transferred to the Methodist church, which maintained control of the institution for the remainder of its existence.

Grenada College was thriving in the early 1900s, when a new administration building, gymnasium, and "Y" building were added to the original campus. In 1925, the catalogue noted that boarding students were limited to two hundred per year. Faculty members numbered eighteen.

The opening of Delta State Teachers College in the late 1920s drew away much of Grenada College's prospective student body. Junior colleges also hurt the school, and the depression was the final blow. In 1932, it was demoted to junior college status and in 1937 it closed for good, its assets absorbed by Millsaps College. The Barwin Hotel occupied the old buildings for several years. A nursing home took over the administration building before razing all of the remaining structures of Grenada College in the 1980s.

Hillman College

Mississippi College claims the honor of being the state's oldest existing college, dating back to its days as Hampstead Academy in 1826. For almost a century, it had a sister institution, Hillman College, existing just a few blocks to the north of MC's campus. All that remains of Hillman are some sections of old foundations, hidden beneath Hillman-Berry Lions Club Park.

Central Female Institute was founded in 1853 by the Central Baptist Association. The first building, which would endure as long as the college existed, was Institute Hall, a frame two-story structure with a gabled roof. After Dr. Walter Hillman began his thirty-eight-year term as president in 1856, a new eighteen-thousand-dollar building was begun, the notes on it due when the roof was finished. The Civil War halted progress on this building when the first-story walls were up; as it never had a roof, the notes never came due. The foundation was later used for the president's home.

Central Female was one of the few schools in Mississippi to continue operations during the Civil War. Following the war, Dr. Hillman bought the property, and in 1891 it was renamed Hillman College. By that time, Adelia Hall was complete, a three-and-a-half-story frame structure with steep gables. It was intended to be a multipurpose facility, as described in the 1889 college catalogue: "Adelia Hall covers a surface of 70 feet in length by 44 feet in breadth, virtually four stories high with an Attic Hall above. The Basement will be used for a dining hall. On the second floor is the Chapel and General Assembly Hall. . . . The third story will be devoted to Dormitories. On the fourth floor there will be two large halls. The one to be used by the Art Department and the other by the Scientific Classes; while in the attic above will be a hall running the entire length of the building, which will be devoted to Calesthenic and other Gymnastic purposes."[23]

After Dr. Hillman's death in 1894, his wife ran the school for two years before selling it to Reverend George Wharton. The Lowrey family, which already owned Blue

Hillman College, ca. 1890. Photo courtesy of MDAH.

Mountain College and ran Mississippi College, took over control of the school in the early 1900s. Lowrey Hall, a fourteen-room dormitory with its own dining hall and art studio, was added. Junior college accreditation was granted by the state.

Hillman thrived until the depression, World War II, and competition from Mississippi College decimated its student base. In 1945, the dwindling school merged with MC, and its buildings were converted to married-student housing for the larger college. As Mississippi College grew and expanded its dormitory stock, Hillman's usefulness waned. Lowrey Hall burned during a 1947 ice storm. The other buildings were abandoned and vandalized. In 1964, the Clinton Lions Club bought the campus for use as a city park. Adelia Hall, the president's house, Institute Hall, and a variety of cottages were demolished. The last remnant of the once-bustling campus was Mary Wyatt Cottage, standing forlornly in a weed-strewn lot until its demolition in 1976.

Lexington Male and Female Academy

William Nichols was an English-born craftsman who had served as the state architect for both North Carolina and Alabama before making his way to Mississippi in

Lexington Male and Female Academy, ca. 1870. Photo courtesy of MDAH.

the 1830s. He would leave a lasting mark on the young state's antebellum architectural legacy, designing and building the Old Capitol, Governor's Mansion, and first State Penitientiary. Moving on to Oxford, he laid out the "circle" at the University of Mississippi and oversaw the construction of the Lyceum and the first campus dormitories.

Nichols then migrated to the central part of Mississippi, where prosperous counties were eager to replace their frontier courthouses and schools with more lasting structures. He designed a massive Greek Revival Yazoo County courthouse, which would be burned during the Civil War. More lasting was his work in Lexington, where he would receive his last commissions and a burial place in the local cemetery.

The Lexington Male and Female Academy had been chartered in the early 1850s. To house it, Nichols built an impressive temple-form school with a Corinthian portico resembling the Greek Tower of the Winds. The school closed during the Civil War and reopened as Central Mississippi Normal College in the years following the war. The academy building was demolished around 1904. The bricks were sold and likely used to help fund the construction of the Lexington public school on the site.

Lowrey Dormitory, Blue Mountain College, ca. 1900. Photo courtesy of Blue Mountain College Archives.

Administration Building, Blue Mountain College, ca. 1940. Photo courtesy of Blue Mountain College Archives.

Early Buildings of Blue Mountain College

On the northernmost edge of Mississippi, the hills of Tippah County rise to resemble Appalachia, with soaring vistas and a bluish tint to the foliage. General Mark Perrin Lowrey, an ordained Baptist minister and veteran of two wars, returned to this corner of the state following Appomattox, dreaming of a more peaceful life and a better future for the young people of the area.

In 1869, General Lowrey saw that dream become a reality. He secured the old Brougher mansion a few miles south of Ripley and organized a college for women. Four years later, Blue Mountain College formally opened, with fifty students boarding at a fee of twelve dollars per month. Their school term lasted forty weeks and was split between the Brougher house and a twenty-four-by-thirty-six-foot log building perched on Blue Mountain.

The college was literally in the middle of nowhere, without even a post office or railroad to connect it to the outside world. General Lowrey dickered with Colonel W. C. Falkner of Ripley, promising the railroad magnate that he would supply a ready stream of highland spring water to the engines if the tracks were laid near the fledgling college. A deal was struck, the lines were run, and the tiny community of Blue Mountain, Mississippi, grew up around the school.

For most of the next century, Blue Mountain was a Lowrey enterprise. Two of General Lowrey's sons succeeded him as president, followed by a grandson. Enrollment grew to several hundred girls by 1900. The first crude log structure disappeared within the walls of a larger, more modern administration building. More and more girls were choosing to board rather than commute, and dormitories were necessary. In keeping with the dominant architecture of the day, they were towered and porched, sprawling houses known affectionately as the B. G., the Lowrey, and the Ray.

The Mississippi Baptist Convention bought the school in 1918, formalizing religious ties that had existed since its formation. In 1928, the old administration building was razed, and a large brick structure took its place. The president's home and several campus buildings, including two cottages and the dormitory called B. G., were destroyed in a Christmas fire that same year.

In 1960, the first president outside of the Lowrey family took charge of Blue Mountain. Opportunities for women had increased dramatically since General Lowrey's day,

Administration Building, Rust College, ca. 1900. Photo courtesy of Chesley Thorne Smith.

and enrollment stabilized at a few hundred students, including male preministerial students. Newer dorms were constructed, and the old one known as Lowrey was demolished for modern development.

Old Rust College Administration Building

During Reconstruction, several colleges for freed slaves opened around Mississippi, including Tougaloo College, Natchez Seminary, and Campbell College. Holly Springs, which had pioneered academic excellence in antebellum north Mississippi, was once again on the cutting edge of providing educational opportunities, this time to blacks who had been long denied the opportunity to learn.

Of the handful of schools which sprang up in Marshall County, the most successful and enduring began as a project of the Freedman's Aid Society of the

Methodist Episcopal Church. Northern missionaries worked with Asbury Church, the first free African-American congregation in Holly Springs, to start a school for all ages, children through adults. Most were illiterate but eager to master basic and more advanced skills.

In 1867, enough money had been raised to construct one building. A ten-thousand-dollar gift from Reverend S. O. Shaw led to the designation of the school as Shaw University. Fifteen years later, it was renamed Rust University to honor the secretary of the Freedman's Aid Society, R. S. Rust of Ohio.

The main building burned in 1888 and was replaced in 1890 with a five-story brick hall dominated by two towers. Administration offices and classrooms were housed in the huge structure, which dominated the skyline behind Holly Springs's courthouse square for fifty years. It was lost to fire in 1940 and replaced by the current McCoy Administration Building.

Mississippi State University's Old Main Dormitory

When the first students arrived at the brand new Mississippi Agricultural and Mechanical College in October 1880, they found themselves homeless. The only dorm was an unfinished and unfurnished shell. The men settled into Starkville boardinghouses and waited until March of the following year to move into the unnamed residence hall. It was an impressive building from the beginning, a brick "U" with 115 rooms. No one dreamed it would grow and metamorphose into the largest dorm under one roof in America, the infamous Old Main.

C. M. Rubush of Vaiden was chosen as the architect to construct the dorm and the first academic building at the fledgling college. For the residence hall, he designed the facade with an imposing Gothic tower, 116 feet high. Typical of its day, the dorm had no running water or indoor toilets; a large cistern between the rear wings of the building provided water to be heated in fireplaces and poured into zinc tubs in each room. Kerosene lamps predated the 1898 installation of electricity. Along with the coal-burning fireplaces, those lamps presented a fire hazard that sent the residents fleeing into the night more than once.

In 1903, with the school's enrollment increasing, a fourth floor was added to the dorm and the dated Gothic tower replaced with a columned, neoclassic facade. An

"Old Main," Mississippi State University, ca. 1890. Photo courtesy of Mary E. Jeffries.

L-shaped dormitory was added to the grounds immediately behind Old Main in 1906 and later enlarged into a full "U." In 1922, it was hooked onto the original structure. The juxtaposed wings didn't even come close to lining up with each other, but no matter. The resulting dipping, curving hallways only added to the excitement of the water hose fights and motorcycle races which would come to symbolize Old Main.

The final building was an enormous 375′ x 266′ hollow square with a 275′ x 172′ inner courtyard. Over five hundred rooms housed nearly fourteen hundred young men. Those in the southwest wing, fondly known as Polecat Alley, shared their rooms with the skunks who scuttled through the labyrinthine basement passages. Moonshine stills in the attic, canoe races down flooded hallways, and frequent fire-related pranks became part of the Old Main legend, home to more than forty thousand men over its seventy-nine-year existence.

With newer dorms rising on campus, little more than the barest maintenance was afforded Old Main from 1922 until 1959. Governor Hugh White was horrified by what he saw on a 1955 campus tour, calling the decrepit behemoth "an eyesore . . . not fit to keep cattle in."[24] Nevertheless, students loved the dorm and filled it every year. They were just back from Christmas vacation when fire broke out on the frigid night of January 23, 1959. After years of false alarms, most ignored the fire bells. When the nine hundred residents realized that a real blaze was racing through the attic, they fled onto the quadrangle with anything they could carry. The fire hoses had been removed by officials weary of water damage from pranksters, and by the time the Starkville Fire Department arrived, the flames were out of control. One student died when he returned to his room for one last load. Everyone else was alerted by classmates pounding on their doors and night watchmen firing pistols in the courtyard.

The residents of Old Main huddled under blankets and watched the dorm collapse. By morning, only a few walls and the columns remained of America's largest dorm. The remnants were demolished and the bricks used in MSU's Chapel of Memories.

Jackson College's and Millsaps College's Founders Hall

Two colleges in Jackson, Millsaps and Jackson State University, can both trace their earliest roots back to one vanished building, Founders Hall. It stood for almost one hundred years on the summit of the ridge now occupied by Millsaps College's campus.

In 1877, the American Baptist Home Mission Society sponsored a school for freed slaves in Natchez, operating out of the old Marine Hospital as Natchez Seminary. It quickly outgrew those limited facilities, and the trustees elected to move to Jackson rather than build a permanent home in Natchez. Fifty-two acres of Judge J. A. P. Campbell's land on the northern edge of Jackson, just across from the State Insane Asylum, were purchased for the newly renamed Jackson College.

When classes began in 1883, there were no true academic or dormitory buildings on the site. Elsinore Mansion, damaged during the Civil War, had been refurbished for use as the college president's home. During the 1883–84 session, classes were held in Mt. Helm Baptist Church, a mission of First Baptist Church. Architect Robert McAllister, using student laborers, began work on a $12,500 three-story brick building to house students and to be used for classes and as an assembly room. It would come to be known as Founders Hall.

Jackson College's enrollment at the North State Street location peaked in 1890–91, with 124 men and 153 women attending classes. The following year, with heavy financial backing from Major Reuben Webster Millsaps, a Methodist school opened close to

Founders' Hall, Millsaps/Jackson College, ca. 1900. Photo courtesy of MDAH.

Jackson College. An offer was made to buy out the black school. President Ayer refused, saying, "I am not interested in selling a college but rather in building a college for underprivileged groups and giving them an opportunity for self-improvement."[25]

Jackson College held out until 1902, when Founders Hall and the campus were sold to Millsaps for forty thousand dollars. The money was used to buy property on Lynch Street, where the small college would grow into Jackson State University. Millsaps expanded around Founders Hall, and over the next seventy years it was used as a dormitory, as a cafeteria, and for classroom space and faculty offices. It was razed in 1973.

Belhaven's Original Campus

Major Reuben Webster Millsaps provided the financial backing for the Methodist Church to charter Millsaps College in 1890. Four years later, his son-in-law, Louis T. Fitzhugh, would open his own school, known as Belhaven in honor of the home where it first held classes.

Fitzhugh had bought the estate of Colonel Jones Hamilton on Boyd Street, near downtown Jackson. Belhaven College for Young Ladies moved into the mansion, described by a visitor in the 1890s as "an elegant, two-story building . . . situated on

Belhaven College, ca. 1900. Photo courtesy of MDAH.

a prominence overlooking a large grove of majestic oaks. . . ."[26] Two buildings were added to complete the campus, and classes began in fall 1894.

An ice storm on February 7, 1895, left water pipes to the campus frozen. Furnaces were going full-blast in the mansion, and a defective flue sent sparks into the wall, igniting the house. With no water available to firemen, it burned in a matter of hours, spreading to include the newer structures as well. Eyewitnesses described the scene: "Beneath the grand old forest trees, outspread upon the soft, green carpet was a conglomerate mass of furniture, china, clothing, books, etc., while fifty girls and twenty teachers moved among them, in the effort to save their all; now dragging heavy trunks across the lawn, now lifting boxes over fences, now again rushing back into the burning houses in search of forgotten treasures—or running to him who stood with aching heart and watched the crowning effort of his life, destroyed."[27]

Fitzhugh was not defeated by the fire. Belhaven moved temporarily to quarters behind the Governor's Mansion. A new group of college structures went up on the old Boyd Street campus and were ready for occupancy by fall 1896. They were a vast improvement over the lost buildings, boasting indoor bathrooms, steam heat, and electricity. The school prospered under Fitzhugh's direction and was sold to J. R. Preston after Fitzhugh's death in 1904.

Preston oversaw the operations of Belhaven until 1910, when the school once again burned. The charter was acquired by the Presbyterian Church, which moved the campus to the "subdivision" which would come to bear the college's name.

Mississippi Heights Academy

A bronze bell on the summit of one of the state's highest hills is the only remnant of Mississippi Heights Academy, a private preparatory school whose story reads like something out of a 1930s movie. No trace is evident of the school building which once topped the summit and was home to hundreds of boys in its forty-year existence.

In 1904, Blue Mountain College had been in business for thirty years, drawing young women to the tiny community in rural Tippah County. Public education, on both the preparatory and college level, was unknown to most of the children in the town. College president B. G. Lowrey spearheaded a drive to raise funds to open a boys' school. His efforts led to the founding of Mississippi Heights Academy, housed in a single brick building at the top of the hill just east of the girls' college.

The school was an immediate success, attracting 60 students in its first year. Its enrollment steadily climbed to a peak of 229 in 1910. In that year, headmaster J. B. Brown limited it to 120 to ensure quality. Four years later, he bought the school outright and served as its guiding light for the next thirty years.

The single building of Mississippi Heights was its academic center. "Prof" Brown was its intellectual and emotional anchor, an educator totally dedicated to his students. Every weekday morning, he rang the tower bell to begin classes. On Sundays, he marched the entire student body to church. He not only recruited boys from Tippah County and northeast Mississippi, but also accepted troubled boys from as far away as Memphis. They boarded in private homes or lived with the Browns. Academic standards were high, and morality was stressed. Sports were emphasized, including wrestling, tennis, and track. When fire broke out in Blue Mountain, the boys of Mississippi Heights made up the entire fire department, falling into a well-rehearsed bucket brigade.

Mississippi Heights Academy, ca. 1930. Photo courtesy of Ripley Public Library.

After World War I, the improving standards of Mississippi's public schools drew many prospective students away. Attendance dwindled, and the depression all but finished the school off. A 1942 stroke left an aged Professor Brown unable to continue, and the academy's doors closed for good. When he died in 1947, the tower bells were rung again and then their cords tied permanently. The building slowly crumbled from neglect. A reporter from Tupelo found it in sad shape in 1954: "Vines cover many of the walls and creep in where window panes are missing; many of the doors sag and a portion of the auditorium ceiling has broken loose at the back."[28]

The old school building was demolished in 1957 and the bronze bell left as a memorial to Mississippi Heights Academy's brief but notable legacy.

Mississippi Heights Academy, ca. 1930. Photo courtesy of Ripley Public Library.

Chapter Two

Hotels and Spas, Springs and Resorts

MISSISSIPPI'S REPUTATION AS THE "HOSPITALITY STATE" rests on deep roots stretching back to colonial days. Long before statehood, a traveler to this far-flung outpost of European imperialism could usually find a dry bed and a stable for his horse, his hosts most likely a lonely farm family with only the rudiments of a roof over their own heads.

That world was a far cry from today's interstate-laced map of high-rise hotels, multimillion-dollar casino developments, and chain motels. But the tone for the state's "open-door" reputation was set two centuries ago, when the first crude cabins popped up along the dirt roads of the wilderness.

In the decades before Mississippi was granted U.S. territorial status, travelers were a rare sight anywhere other than along the lower Mississippi River valley. Flatboaters docking at Natchez would abandon their crude rafts beneath the bluffs and set out for home on the old Indian trails that made up the Natchez Trace. They found an occasional "stand," or tavern, along the road, welcome respites from sleeping on the forest floor.

The only extant Natchez Trace stand in Mississippi is Mount Locust, probably one of the oldest of these early "hotels" and characteristic of the accommodations offered in the late 1700s and early 1800s. Typically of log construction, often bisected by a cooling "dogtrot" passage between rooms, the better ones boasted plank floors and glass windows, real beds, and decent food. More primitive stands were little more than huts with dirt floors and cornshuck mattresses. But to the "Kaintucks" trudging home from the river, any shelter was better than none.

During Mississippi's territorial period, from 1798 to 1817, the Natchez region reigned supreme in population, culture, and politics. Logically, it also offered the first

Wesson Hotel
(See page 62.)

true inns in Mississippi. Those beneath the bluff, catering to the rough-and-tumble boatmen, were little more than saloons with upstairs dormitories. Above the bluffs, the southern terminus of the Trace attracted several true tavernkeepers, offering food and a more socially acceptable lodging. Connelly's Tavern, King's Tavern, and White Horse Tavern enjoyed a booming business during the heyday of the Trace.

Rural Mississippians, jealous of Natchez's dominance in the old Southwest, finagled the transfer of the state capital six miles north to the hamlet of Washington. Elected representatives from the remote corners of the territory traveled for days to reach the capital. They required extended accommodations before heading home, and enterprising tavernkeepers quickly appeared to fill that need. By 1805,Washington boasted three hotels and a scattering of houses. Three years later, there were thirty homes, three taverns, and, of necessity, a jail.

One of the taverns was built by Ebenezer Rees, no earlier than 1801. The frame residence, which came to be known as Assembly Hall, was rented to the territorial legislature from 1808 until 1811. It served triple duty as the statehouse, a drinking spot, and a boardinghouse.

Natchezians wasted little time grieving for the loss of the political crowd. Cotton and steamboats were transforming the once-shabby river town into a mecca for millionaires. As the territory became a state, these newly minted "nabobs" demanded more luxurious accommodations for their guests. Leaving the crude wooden taverns to riverboatmen, the well-healed visitor disembarking from paddlewheelers took a carriage up the bluff to Parker's Hotel, described in the 1830s as "probably the best accommodations to be had,"[1] or the Mansion House, "an extensive and commodious brick edifice said to be one of the best hotels in the southwest."[2] Along with the Mercer House, these grand hotels offered fine dining, reading rooms and ballrooms. Galleries encircled the Mansion House, and Parker's was acclaimed as "a handsome, costly and very extensive building, three stories in height, with a stuccoed front, in imitation of granite, and decidedly the largest edifice in the city."[3]

For thirty years, Natchez and Adams County were the undisputed center of Mississippi's cultural life. But as the Indian treaties of the 1820s and 1830s opened up the interior of Mississippi for settlement, it became obvious that the capital city would need to be in a more central location than Washington or Natchez. A bluff above the swampy Pearl River was chosen and named Jackson. A grid of streets was laid out and a small statehouse built on Capitol Street. The town's promoters eagerly awaited the influx of politicians, money, and opportunity. Once a year, the legislators appeared, but they fled the swampy, mosquito-infested village as soon as their business was finished. The available accommodations were notoriously inadequate, and businesses were not drawn to a town which was largely deserted for much of the year. Legislators grumbled and jockeyed for removal of the capital to their hometowns, and Jackson was all but doomed. Only a legislative threat to abandon the city altogether spurred those devoted to its future to work on building a real city.

As Mississippi grew and developed into one of the country's wealthiest young states, the prosperity slowly trickled down to Jackson. Recognizing a ready-made, captive clientele in the legislators, several boardinghouses had opened by the 1830s. Only one was a true hotel in any sense of the word. The Eagle Hotel rose on Amite Street, just across from the planned new statehouse. By the standards of the day, the hostelry was more than acceptable, but this was still the edge of the frontier and the hotel's reputation reflected that. Judge J. T. Wharton described his brief visit to the Eagle in 1837: "After supper, curiosity led me to take a stroll up State Street to the Eagle Hotel at the northeast corner of State and Amite Streets. There was an underground, dark and cavernous saloon, fitly located as all such 'air holes of hell' may be supposed to be. It was crowded with a gay and festive party, making night hideous with their bacchanalian revel."[4] Despite Judge Wharton's misgivings about the Eagle, it was considered the capital city's finest offering on and off for twenty years. It was briefly the home of Jackson College, housed several offices, and reopened as a hotel in 1846.

Far south of Jackson, Mississippi's Gulf Coast was awakening and attracting city-weary travelers from New Orleans and Mobile. It was not yet the "Riviera of the South," but the opening of the Pass Christian Hotel in 1836 foreshadowed that legacy. This early resort started as a simple beach hotel and grew to include a dining room, ballroom, billiard room, bowling alley, and stables. Wings were added to the original hotel block, culminating in a U-shaped complex with hundreds of rooms. In 1849, the South's first regatta sailed from its pier, drawing competitors from Bay St. Louis, Biloxi, Mississippi City, Mobile, New Orleans, Pensacola, and Pascagoula. The event was an enormous success, and from that meeting the Pass Christian Yacht Club was born, second in longevity only to New York City's.

Pass Christian was one of the "Six Sisters," a string of holiday hideaways for the wealthy of New Orleans and Mobile. Shieldsboro, Mississippi City, Biloxi, Ocean Springs, and Pascagoula established their reputation as cool, oak-shaded stopovers for steamboat passengers along the coast. Harriet Porter's beachfront Ocean Springs Hotel gave its name to the village which grew up around it. The Magnolia Hotel in Biloxi was a forerunner of dozens of hostelries which would become synonymous with that town.

In antebellum days, the Gulf Coast pulled visitors from the major cities in neighboring states. Mississippians further inland preferred to spend their days, and often weeks or entire seasons, at "spas" or "healing springs" which were popping up all over the countryside. Reverend Preston Cooper followed what he believed to be divine urging to dig seventy-five feet through solid rock near Raymond, finally hitting a spring that "stinketh mightily."[5] When a neighbor suffering some incurable malady improved after a desperate sampling of the rancid water, the preacher was in business. Cooper's Well grew into an enormous resort, accommodating five hundred guests at a time who flocked in from all over the state and the South to indulge in the restorative springs.

Artesian Springs, north of Canton, was the chief competitor to Cooper's Well. An 1850 ad in the *Madisonian* touted "buildings sufficiently spacious to accommodate 500 persons"[6] on the main stagecoach line from Pickens to Thomastown. Dances and barbecues were the preferred entertainment for those fortunate enough to loll away their days at these posh resorts.

Political rallies also drew thousands to Cooper's Well and Artesian Springs. Many of those politicians were promoting secession by the mid-to-late 1850s. They led Mississippi out of the Union in 1861, but the initial euphoria of rebellion and war soon gave way to harsh economic reality, as disposable income dried up and men went off to fight. The spas closed, and the coast hotels lost much of their steamboat traffic.

When war swept into Mississippi in earnest, the great hotels and resorts of the state were no more immune to destruction than private homes or public buildings. Jackson's Bowman House, successor to the Eagle, was headquarters for Confederate generals in May 1863; the rooms there were occupied by Union officers less than a week later. It escaped the wholesale destruction of Jackson by Union troops in May, only to burn accidentally in June. A competitor, the Confederate House, known to be "constantly thronged with quartermaster, commissaries, paymasters and a horde of gamblers"[7] was probably torched by disgruntled Union soldiers, insulted by the owner's southern sympathies. Cooper's Well's magnificent main building was also a casualty of the Vicksburg campaign, burned by Union soldiers after the Battle of Raymond.

The stark ruins of the Bowman House stood as tragic reminders of the price of war until the mid-1870s. Its walls finally came down just as Mississippi was emerging from the dark days of Reconstruction. With the economy recovering and North-South relations thawing, Mississippi slowly edged back into the hospitality business. New spas and springs joined the rebuilt Cooper's Well. Allison's Wells, Castalian Springs, and Lafayette Springs beckoned health-conscious Mississippians during the long, hot summers.

Railroads finally linked Mobile and New Orleans, bringing a burst of resort hotel construction in Pass Christian. Described as "the beautiful little garden spot, named on the map as Pass Christian, although it might well be called Paradise, so beautiful is everything surrounding the place,"[8] Pass Christian capitalized most quickly and effectively on the tourist boom. The old Pass Christian Hotel, which had early on set the standard for luxury along the coast, had been sold to the Christian Brothers Order for use as a college. Replacing it to handle the influx of sunseekers was the fabled Mexican Gulf Hotel, "by long odds the finest hotel architecturally on the entire coast . . . greatly envied by many of the other hotel keepers of the coast."[9] The overflow from trains bringing northerners in the winter and southerners in the summer filtered out to Lynne Castle, Gray Castle, the New Magnolia, and Inn-by-the-Sea.

Mississippi City was Pass Christian's neighbor to the east and home to the Gulf View Hotel, the first coast resort to reopen following the Civil War. Its "mile-long" pier jutting into the Mississippi Sound was a landmark never equalled. The coastline between Pass Christian and Mississippi City was largely empty until Joseph T. Jones, a Pennsylvania native and Union army veteran, completed the long-awaited Gulf and Ship Island Railroad from Jackson to the coast. Bringing the rails in at the point where the Mississippi Sound would be dredged for a deepwater port, Jones almost single-handedly created the new city of Gulfport as the twentieth century dawned. Gulfport quickly grew into the world's largest exporter of yellow pine lumber, and businessmen and vacationers flocked to Jones's Great Southern Hotel, a $250,000, 250-room wonder. Running hot and cold water, baths shared between only two rooms, a "complete system of sewerage carrying all waste one-half mile into the Gulf," and a "fine orchestra provid[ing] music at the hotel everyday" made the twenty-six-hour train trip from Chicago to Gulfport worthwhile to hundreds of snow-weary northerners.[10]

The first three decades of the new century were prosperous times for many Mississippians. They had access to railroads, automobiles, and slowly improving highways. Tastes were changing. Spas gradually slipped out of vogue, and the aging resorts of

Pass Christian fell one by one to fires and hurricanes. New hotels, larger and more modern, sprang up to take their place. Capitalizing on the proximity of the Old Spanish Trail Highway, a nationwide asphalt ribbon connecting San Diego and St. Augustine, a group of New Orleans businessmen bankrolled the towering pink Pine Hills Hotel. Its tree-lined drives led directly off the highway in 1926, winding through golf courses and residential developments to the north shore of Bay St. Louis. Straddling the border between Gulfport and Biloxi, the two-million-dollar Edgewater Gulf was larger than any hotel yet built in Mississippi, but it was soon challenged by the Buena Vista, the coast's first "Pacific-style" resort.

The capital city was not to be outdone by the Gulf Coast. Dotting downtown Jackson at one time were the Heidelberg, with its famous rooftop ballroom; the Walthall; the Edwards (later the King Edward); and the Robert E. Lee. Smaller towns had their railroad hotels and fashionable downtown inns, like Greenwood's Irving, West Point's Henry Clay, and Brookhaven's Inez. They were the social and political centers of society, the place where anyone of importance could generally be located and much of the business of a community was conducted.

After World War II, the days of Mississippi's great hotels were numbered. Interstate highways bypassed many Main Streets, pulling business away from the old institutions and attracting chain motels. Railroads no longer brought trainloads of customers to downtown hostelries, and the Gulf Coast gradually lost its tourist business to newer resorts and whiter beaches in Florida.

The spa hotels were the first to go. Long abandoned and crumbling, they either disappeared into the encroaching forests or burned down. Cooper's Well burned again in 1942, and the once proud Artesian Springs was converted to a family home before being abandoned altogether.

The big hotels fared no better. The Heidelberg was demolished to make room for a Capitol Street parking lot. The King Edward, once the home of political intrigue and deal-making that could rival the state capitol itself, was shuttered and doomed to house only pigeons and vagrants as it gradually crumbled.

Mississippi's once vibrant Gulf Coast saw its convention and resort trade depart for the newer hotels along Florida's shoreline. Thousands of south Mississippians, eager for progress but mourning the impending loss of an old friend, gathered on a humid Sunday morning in 1971 to watch the controlled demolition of the Edgewater Gulf. It would take several attempts and more than eight hundred pounds of explosives to finally bring the grande dame down, clearing the way for a mall. Destruction of the "Pink Palace," the long-abandoned Pine Hills Hotel near Pass Christian, would be no easier. Once the pride of the entire Gulf Coast, it had functioned as a hotel for only three short years, 1926–29. For most of the next half-century, it sat empty, surviving even a direct hit from Hurricane Camille. When demolition crews arrived in 1981, they expected an easy job. Their iron ball battered the tower three times without making a dent. The 180 rooms were finally dismantled by hand, leaving only an overgrown road and a rotting pier to mark this apex of Mississippi's hospitality history.

Assembly Hall

Southwest Mississippi was a hotbed of political intrigue in the early 1800s. Republican factions debated Federalist diehards, country planters resented the nabobs of Natchez, and newcomers were jockeying for power in the territorial frontier. When Thomas Jefferson appointed W. C. C. Claiborne as territorial governor in 1802, one of Claiborne's first actions was to move the territorial capital from Natchez to the Republican stronghold of Washington, a tiny village six miles to the northeast.

Described by a visitor in 1803 as an "indifferent looking little place in which scarcely one house was finished,"[11] Washington was not an impressive capital city. Governor Claiborne moved his own residence there and was soon followed by others eager to be close to the center of political power. By 1808, it was a respectable small town, with thirty homes, a store, three taverns, and the ubiquitous jail.

One of the taverns was an unassuming two-story clapboard dwelling owned by Charles DeFrance. Its interior was typical of these combination bar/boardinghouse establishments of the day, with exposed ceiling beams and walls of horizontal tongue-and-groove boards. A central brick chimney provided heat; a wide front gallery lent ventilation on hot summer days.

Washington never claimed an official government building. The legislature rented the tavern from DeFrance from 1808 to 1811 and held their sessions in the taproom. When Mississippi became a state and the new capital city of Jackson was designated, Washington was left behind. It withered and all but disappeared. The old tavern, ever after known as Assembly Hall, survived as an inn and later a private home for another 170 years. It was empty and delapidated when it was destroyed by fire in the late 1980s.

Assembly Hall, ca. 1985.
Photo courtesy of MDAH.

Assembly Hall, ca. 1985.
Photo courtesy of MDAH.

Eagle Hotel and Bowman House

The northeast corner of Amite and State streets, immediately north of Mississippi's Old Capitol, was the first center of hotel hospitality in Jackson. Abram DeFrance opened the Eagle Hotel there in the early 1820s, capitalizing on the need legislators had for a decent place to stay during the political season. While it may have been nicer than the average boardinghouse or tavern in Jackson, the Eagle still betrayed its frontier origins, described by a visitor in 1837 as "an underground, dark and cavernous saloon."[12]

The Eagle stood for more than thirty years, even serving briefly as the home of Jackson College in 1845. It was delapidated and empty when torn down to make room for the Bowman House in 1857. The Bowman was an up-to-date, four-story brick hotel with approximately one hundred rooms. It quickly gained a reputation as Mississippi's "largest and most commodious hotel,"[13] attracting the elite and important visitors of the day.

In the spring of 1863, the Bowman House played host to a meeting of Confederate generals desperate to save Jackson and Vicksburg from Grant's approaching troops. Just a week later, Union officers met in the same location after their successful occupation of Jackson. Generals Grant, Sherman, and McPherson enjoyed the rare treat of having a nice room and fine food as they plotted the impending siege of Vicksburg. They left the hotel unharmed and headed on to the front lines. With Jackson back in Confederate hands, the Bowman House burned to the ground less than a month later, under circumstances never fully explained. The *Jackson Daily News* reported the loss:

> In yesterday's edition we stopped the press to announce the destruction of this, the only hotel in Jackson. The alarm of fire was given at twenty minutes past 3 o'clock, Wednesday morning, and so rapid was the progress of the flames that in fifteen minutes from its discovery the entire roof of both wings fell in, and ten minutes later the upper story was in flames. The fire originated in the top of the house, under the roof, as there was no fire in the upper story when discovered by the sentinel. Rumors have been circulated that one or two persons perished in the flames, but it is contradicted by the officers of the house. It has been conjectured to be the work of an incendiary, but we are inclined to attribute it to accident. The loss of this hotel is a great public calamity, especially as it is impossible to rebuild for the present. The

Bowman House, ca. 1863. Photo courtesy of MDAH.

Ruins of Bowman House, ca. 1870. Photo courtesy of MDAH.

> building was insured for $25,000 and the furniture for $10,000. All the furniture and other preparations of the establishment were lost. We understand that the loss of Messrs. Daniel and Co., the proprietors, in this respect was $20,000.[14]

With much of Jackson in ashes and the subsequent preoccupation with war and Reconstruction, the barren ruins of the Bowman House stood for thirteen years. In a postwar photo of the Old Capitol, a partially collapsed wall juts up in the corner like a sentinel. The owners of the property squabbled and fought until 1876, when the remains were finally pulled down and the bricks sold for salvage. The site later served as the home of Daniel Wilkinson and is now occupied by the former Standard Oil Building.

Confederate House

The only visual evidence that the Confederate House ever existed in west Jackson is the line drawing from an illustrated newspaper of 1863 showing the building engulfed in flames. Little is known of its reputation before the war, but it became a mainstay for southern troops in the days before Jackson fell to Union occupation. A member of the Fourteenth Mississippi Infantry remembered the hotel: "The Confederate House in west Jackson was constantly thronged with quartermasters, commissaries, paymasters and a horde of gamblers, with bogus passes, filled the hotels."[15]

The drawing of the Confederate House illustrates a three-story building with elaborate galleries on each level of one facade. A square cupola crowns the roof. To the side, a pagoda-like building of uncertain purpose is also in flames.

Much of Jackson was in ruins after Federal occupation in mid-May 1863. Some of the destruction was wrought by Confederates eager to prevent supplies from falling into Union hands. Some was accidental, and only a portion was due to northern enmity. The Confederate Hotel was likely a victim of the latter. General William T Sherman recalled, in later years, the circumstances surrounding the hotel's loss:

> I never found out exactly who set it on fire, but was told that in one of our batteries were some officers and men who had been made prisoners at Shiloh, with Prentiss's division, and had been carried past Jackson in a railroad-train; they had been permitted to go to this very

Confederate House, ca. 1863. Photo courtesy of MDAH.

> hotel for supper, and had nothing to pay but greenbacks, which were refused, with insult, by this . . . landlord. These men, it was said, had quietly and stealthily applied the fire underneath the hotel just as we were leaving town.[16]

Sherman neglects to mention whether these men were ever proven to be the culprits or received any reprimand. The hotel was never rebuilt and even its exact location is a mystery.

Pass Christian Hotel and New Magnolia Hotel

The village of Pass Christian, an easy steamboat journey from New Orleans, early on established itself as the retreat of choice from the heat and disease of the Crescent City. Wealthy Louisianans built palatial summer homes along the coastline and considered themselves dual citizens of Mississippi and Louisiana. When the Pass Christian

Pass Christian Hotel, ca. 1840. Photo courtesy of MDAH.

Hotel opened in 1836, the comforts of this coastal paradise were available for those looking for a temporary getaway rather than a second home, and business boomed.

By 1839, the original Pass Christian Hotel had been enlarged to include a dining room, ballroom, billiard hall, and nine-pin alley. Stables and bathing houses were scattered on the grounds and along the shoreline. Families were welcomed, separated from the single men who resided in the "Texas wing," basically a huge dormitory.

Entrepreneur R. H. Montgomery purchased the hotel in 1847. It would come to acquire his name, deservedly so considering the innovations he brought to Gulf Coast hospitality. In July 1849, Montgomery invited sailors from all along the Mississippi coast, Pensacola, Mobile, and New Orleans to participate in a regatta. The success of this event led to the creation of the Pass Christian Yacht Club, the second oldest in the country after New York City's.

Montgomery continued to expand the Pass Christian Hotel, transforming it into a sprawling U-shaped complex with hundreds of rooms. A hurricane temporarily shut it

New Magnolia Hotel, ca. 1900. Photo courtesy of Pass Christian Historical Society (from the Bruce Stinson Collection).

down in 1855, and the Civil War closed it for good. Following the war, the Christian Brothers Order purchased it for use as a college. With the completion of railroad service into Pass Christian and the resurgence of the tourist business, it reopened as a hotel in the 1870s, only to burn in 1877.

The site was vacant until 1886, when the Pass Christian Institute, a girls' school, opened on the lot. It struggled along for eight years. As more and more vacationers crowded off the trains at Pass Christian, two enterprising hoteliers bought the school and converted it into the New Magnolia Hotel. As if inspired by its illustrious predecessor, the New Magnolia quickly gained a reputation as Pass Christian's premier resort. "It is a building of spacious halls, wide staircases, finely furnished parlors, airy rooms, beautiful dining halls and roomy verandas extend[ing] entirely around the edifice. . . . In the ten acres of lawns and play ground may be found swings, hammocks, croquet, lawn tennis and many other games for the benefit of the guests and which may be indulged in during the hottest hours of the day, owing to the fact that the grounds are well-shaded with stately oak, magnolia, sweet gum and other ornamental trees which throw a delightful shade over the entire place, while there is scarcely a moment when there are not refreshing breezes blowing in from off the waters." [17]

Each of the forty "apartments" in the New Magnolia could be rented for $2.00–$2.50 per day. This included access to the wharf and bathing pavilion in the gulf. Guests also enjoyed vegetables raised on the grounds by the staff.

The New Magnolia's days on the coast were limited. Just twenty-one years after it opened, it burned to the ground on April Fools' Day in 1915.

Cooper's Well

The story of Cooper's Well, one of Mississippi's premier nineteenth-century spas, begins with a preacher who couldn't sleep in peace. His visions led him to dig and keep digging until he hit the waterspout that would lead to one of the state's most spectacular success stories.

Reverend Preston Cooper bought the rocky hillside acreage outside Raymond in 1837 for "a small sum of money."[18] It was not prime land and "was only considered valuable for its salubrious and romantic situation and desirable locality for a quiet and peaceful country residence."[19] The preacher elected to build a house at the top of one of the hillsides on his new land, but this left him without ready access to water. He hired a well digger, who quit in exasperation after hitting solid rock about thirty feet down. Cooper settled for a cistern and thought no more about the well.

Reverend Cooper's satisfaction with his water situation was short-lived. He began having strange dreams. "One night as I lay on my bed wrapped up in a peaceful and quiet sleep, induced by a consciousness of being at peace with all men, I dreamed that I saw the figure of a man with a familiar face stand before me, and when I looked, the man said. 'Cooper, resume the digging of your well; much depends upon it; it is all important that you do it; see that you do it!' and vanished. So plain was the dream that when I awoke . . . I could scarcely persuade myself that it had been a dream. This occurred in Vicksburg, in 1838, while I was there preaching, and some time after the work on the well had been given up, and all idea of prosecuting it had been abandoned."[20]

Cooper tried to shrug off the disturbing vision, with no success. "A few nights after this the same vision appeared again to me with the same face repeating the same words . . . . It occurred again and again for months with scarcely an intermission of a week . . . until at the end of five months I began to feel that there must be something more than mere association in this singular affair. After pondering the matter well I concluded it was my duty to resume work."[21]

He hired another digger, who tunneled through a solid nine-foot-thick rock before hitting even harder layers. Cooper gave him permission to give up and assumed he had satisfied his dream visitor. "Thus matters stood for nearly two months when the same dreams returned exactly as they had before . . . Thus it pursued me almost nightly until I determined to employ a third digger. I did so and employed a man who, after immense labor penetrated through the rock, almost solid for thirty feet further, and then declared it was not only useless but foolish and gave up the job. The expense being heavy and I being poor, I did not insist on his continuing, so suspended the work for the third time."[22]

By this time, the Reverend Cooper and his dreams and his indomitable rocks were bordering on folly. He left on a circuit-riding tour, and once again had a nocturnal visitor. "[S]uddenly one night, the same familiar face, as a messenger from Heaven—or a meddler from Hell—in the stillness of the midnight hour, stood before me and in the more commanding voice than used before, said: 'Cooper, you must finish the well, you must employ the fourth digger; much depends upon it; see that you do it!' . . . I also dreamed before I awoke that I employed the fourth digger and that he did obtain water, that I saw it got and that the man said, when he obtained it, 'I have got water but it stinketh mightily, so that you cannot use it.' I awoke troubled and perplexed."[23]

Obviously, the preacher was not going to get a sound night's sleep until he struck water. He hired well digger number four, who arrived on a Tuesday and set to work. By Friday afternoon, all the neighbors had gathered to watch his progress. "My neighbors . . . expected a disappointment. I expected a realization of my dreams. At this time I was leaning on the windlass looking down into the well; anxiety was at its highest point. A few moments later the digger struck his mattock into the crevice of a rock and water appeared. It looked to me like a bright coin at the bottom of the well and in answer to my question, 'What is that?' he said, 'It is water, but it stinketh mightily, it stinketh so bad you can never use it.' Thus, at a few minutes after four on Friday, the sixteenth day of September, 1841, was realized my dream."[24]

Reverend Cooper's premonitions had paid off, but the water was foul and disappointing. Stories vary, but either a neighbor's mule or a local doctor drank it and was

Cooper's Well, ca. 1850. Photo courtesy of Old Courthouse Museum, Vicksburg.

instantly cured of some unknown malady. Word spread, and soon people from all over Mississippi were on the reverend's doorstep demanding water. His enterprising brother-in-law, Inman Williams, who had no doubt enjoyed laughing at his kinsman's vain efforts for four years, bought a half-interest in the property and built a hotel, installing himself as manager. In 1850, Reverend Cooper sold out the remainder of his interest to another brother-in-law, John Epps. A stock company, known as Cooper's Well Company, was formed to construct a hotel and outbuildings. One of the managers was a character by the name of General MacMackin, who made a show of announcing the nightly bill of fare in rhyme.

Guests streamed in from all over the South, eager for the waters, the hospitality, the food, and the ever-present political undercurrents. Jefferson Davis and Governor Foote debated before an 1851 crowd of several thousand Mississippians, undoubtedly eager to see if the two statesmen would once again exchange blows, as they had in Washington, D.C. An 1859 letter by the unidentified "B" could have been used as advertising fodder:

> A week has slipped rapidly away at this delightful watering place since your correspondent alighted from the bright-red stage coach which brought him up so comfortably from the Terry

> depot on the Jackson Railroad, and when he took his first cool drink of the renowned chalybeate water at the well . . . There has been a larger proportion of New Orleans people at the Well this season than there has ever been before, which is to be accounted for by the fact of the railroad connection. One has only to jump in the cars at six o'clock at Tivoli Circle, and after a pleasant trip of thirty miles across the Lake, a nice dinner at Brookhaven, handing in the checks at Terry's and the nice mule team is trotting you past the cotton fields of Governor Brown and others, and while the band is playing the sunset airs, and the ladies and gentlemen are taking their evening stroll to the Springhouse, you are shown to a room by the attentive gentleman in charge of the office . . . You can not imagine how refreshing it is, these beautiful days and lovely moonlight nights, seated out upon the balconies . . .[25]

Just a few years later, the halls of Cooper's Well would be filled with Confederate officers enjoying the last peaceful days before war tore central Mississippi apart. The hotel was lost to fire after the Battle of Raymond, and for several years only the well marked the site of the great hotel. A smaller hotel was built, but it also burned and left those determined to come for the waters no choice but to camp out. In 1884, the site was sold to the Spengler family, who would own and manage the spa for most of the next fifty years. The largest and grandest of the three hotels on the site was built in 1884, a long, galleried, multichimneyed building topped with multiple spires, capable of accommodating more than five hundred visitors. Chandeliers from the steamboat *Natchez* hung in the huge dining hall. A two-story cypress pavilion went up over the famous well, still pumping out its malodorous miracle water. Brochures touted "a full corps of attentive attendants [who] are kept busy at all hours drawing by windlass and pumps fresh supplies of water which is handed around to the guests."[26] For those who couldn't make the trip to Raymond, Cooper's Well would ship them bottles or five-gallon demijohns of the liquid. But the "waters" weren't the only attraction at the resort. The billiard hall and bowling lanes ran nonstop, and hired cardsharps kept the action going in the gambling hall.

Cooper's Well boomed until the early 1920s, when it was sold briefly to a group of New Orleans businessmen. The Spengler family took over again in 1923, and tried valiantly to keep going during the dark days of the depression. In 1940, the hotel closed for good and burned to the ground shortly afterwards. The land was given over to cattle ranching and farming, and gradually the woods reclaimed the site. Only the cypress pavilion remained to mark the site of Reverend Cooper's long-sought well, and it, too, burned in the 1970s. Cooper's Well was all but forgotten and in danger of being paved over when it was saved in 1999 by owners who plan to make it into an educational campground.

Artesian Springs

With former Indian lands going for $1.25 per acre and cotton fueling an economic boom, 1830s Mississippi was rapidly transformed from a sparsely settled wilderness into a state of small towns and prosperous planters. James Gillespie was one who came to the central part of the state and purchased a large tract in Madison County. He cleared land for a home and set about digging a well for his family. What he found was mineral-rich artesian springs, and within a few years his water was renowned for its "curative" powers.

All across Mississippi, spa hotels were springing up, both for relaxation and medicinal purposes. The Artesian Springs Hotel was one of the largest, described in an 1850 *Madisonian* ad as "buildings sufficiently spacious to accommodate 500 persons."[27] Large central hostelries housed guest rooms, a ballroom, tenpin alley, and a bar. Surrounding these were double cottages and numerous well houses. Well located on the stagecoach road between Pickens and Thomastown, the Artesian Springs stayed packed year-round. Elizabeth Hatheway, who must have been used to luxury and elegance in her role as governess at Annandale plantation, was still in awe of the grand hotel after an 1855 visit: "I am just back, from a most delightful excursion to Artesian Wells, about forty miles from here . . . There are four bored wells . . . all in a row, not two feet apart, all possessing different properties. There are three immense lath and plaster hotels . . . neatly white washed and the long half mile of open galleries are delightful, so altogether we found as much amusement as could be crammed into the space of three days."[28] Political rallies were common, such as a July 4, 1854, celebration that lasted all night, complete with multiple orations and a dusk to dawn ball.

During the Civil War, the main buildings burned. The site remained popular with picnickers and tent campers despite the lack of formal accommodations. In 1891, John Livelar and Angelo Garbarino of Canton built a new twenty-two-room hotel and uncapped the famous wells. These two men were at odds from the beginning. The new Artesian Springs had been open only a few days when a furious argument

Artesian Springs, ca. 2000. Photo by the author.

between the proprietors led to a complete rupture of the business arrangement. The hotel, fully furnished and stocked with fine linens, china, and silverware, was shuttered. It sat unused for thirteen years, until Lonnie Meeks of Attala County purchased it in 1904. He had no intention of reopening the spa, but rather moved his wife and twelve children into it as their new home. The family and its descendants lived there until 1964. It now sits empty and sagging, barely visible through the forest closing about it. A few well houses and brick wells are scattered through the woods, the only evidence of James Gillespie's miraculous find a century and a half ago.

Mexican Gulf Hotel

When the New Orleans-to-Mobile railroad was completed in 1870, Pass Christian was ideally situated to benefit from the surge of Reconstruction-weary, newly prosperous

Mexican Gulf Hotel, ca. 1890. Drawing courtesy of Pass Christian Historical Society.

tourists looking for sun and relaxation. Its beautiful shoreline and live oak–shaded streets were a perfect draw for those who would come to regard this as the "American Riviera."

The Mexican Gulf was one of the first "modern" hotels to open and court the tourist trade. Completed in 1883, at the then-astronomical cost of $105,000, its 250 rooms were "supplied with all modern conveniences such as electric bells, gas and steam heat."[29] Northerners flocked in during the winters, fleeing the snow in Chicago, St. Louis, and Cincinnati. In summer, New Orleanians and Mississippians filled the hotel. An 1895 promotional brochure touted the advantages of a Mexican Gulf stay in glowing terms:

> This beautiful house is by long odds the finest hotel architecturally on the entire coast, and its interior decorations and furnishings are beautiful in the extreme, so much so in fact as to cause the management of this house to be greatly envied by many of the other hotel keepers on the coast . . . The immense office from which the grand staircase runs to the floor above . . . is the finest on the coast. The office and staircase are carpeted with heavy velvet Brussels into

Mexican Gulf Hotel, ca. 1890. Photo courtesy of Pass Christian Historical Society (from the Bruce Stinson Collection).

which the feet seem to sink as the guests walk across to the dining room or ladies parlor . . . There are two enormous open fireplaces here, on which logs are placed in the chilly winter evenings, which throw out a grateful warmth and light which reflected on the bright colored carpets and hangings make the place look cheery and homelike . . . Taken all in all the Mexican Gulf Hotel is one of the finest places in the entire South at which to pass either a summer or winter vacation, and the invalid could not find a better place in which to build up the constitution . . . It is just such a place that the tired businessman can find rest and recreation from the cares of city life.[30]

The main building of this mecca was a sprawling, towered three-story Queen Anne structure, surrounded by several cottages and outbuildings. For three dollars to five dollars per day, guests enjoyed spacious rooms and lawns "kept in splendid trim and shaded by stately live oak trees, under whose spreading branches seats are placed." [31]

The Mexican Gulf welcomed thousands of guests during its thirty-four-year history. President Wilson dined in the two-hundred-seat dining room during his recuperative visit to Pass Christian in 1913. The hotel weathered several hurricanes and underwent a modernizing renovation in 1916. Staff members were preparing for its winter season reopening when a third-floor fire raced out of control, destroying the main building. Only the cottages and live oaks were left to mark the site of one of Pass Christian's legendary tourist draws.

Wesson Hotel

On the map of Mississippi, there's a mysterious notch carved into the boundary line between Copiah and Lincoln counties. It dips southward just far enough to incorporate the town of Wesson into Copiah County and then loops back to the logical latitude. It's an aberration with a story hidden deep in the Reconstruction years of the 1870s.

Colonel James Madison Wesson was a successful Choctaw County mill owner when the Civil War started. His manufacturing facility was torched by Union troops, and in 1864 he chose a plot of land a few miles north of Brookhaven on which to rebuild. The Mississippi Manufacturing Company was off the ground and running by 1866, and with it the little company town of Wesson, named for the man who built the cotton mill and seventy-six company houses. He sold some of his property, including the site of a hotel, with the stipulation that the deed would revert to him if alcoholic beverages were sold on the premises. Taking his prohibitionist fervor one step further, he lobbied the legislature to tuck Wesson into dry Copiah County rather than wet and wicked Lincoln County. Thus, the illogical tab on the map that still exists today.

In 1870, Colonel Wesson sold out to two New Orleans businessmen, Captain William Oliver and John T. Hardy. Their mill burned just three years later, but they were not deterred. Edmund Richardson, a fabulously wealthy and successful Delta planter and cotton broker, joined their partnership, and the company was reorganized as Mississippi Mills. By 1887, their three massive mill buildings claimed the title as the largest manufacturing institution south of the Ohio River, employing several thousand south Mississippians in producing fine cotton known as "Mississippi silk." The mills had their own power plant, a true novelty in that day and age, and power was supplied not only to the machinery but to the town of Wesson. People from all over Mississippi flocked to see the electric lights of Wesson.

John P. Richardson, son of Edmund Richardson and son-in-law of William Oliver, built the Richardson House in 1877 as a replacement for the 1864 hotel, which had burned. It was ideally situated just a hundred yards or so from the busy Illinois Central

Wesson Hotel, ca. 1930. Photo courtesy of MDAH.

depot. Two stories with a large attic, the frame building was raised on brick piers. Its twenty-eight rooms were arranged in a U-shaped plan with an adjoining kitchen wing. Galleries stretched across the front and rear facades, overlooking a courtyard with a pagoda-styled well house. In the middle of the attic roof was a large peaked gable with a window, the ideal lookout point for gamblers frequenting what was reported to be the largest casino operation between New Orleans and Memphis.

The Richardson House, or Wesson Hotel, as it came to be known, was renowned throughout the South for its meals and exceptionally comfortable rooms. A typical room's furnishings were described in an 1882 insurance report: "[A] bedroom set consisting of bedstead. Dresser Washstand Table Towel Rack. 2 Rockers BedSprings & mattress chamber & Toilet sets 2 lamps and 2 Trunks in the Wesson Hotel known as the Richardson House."[32] Salesmen, or "drummers," who flocked into Wesson to stock the several general stores and buy from the mills, filled the rooms nightly. They displayed their wares in a large first-floor room known until the building's demise as the "sample room."

The Wesson Hotel thrived along with Mississippi Mills and the town. But when the Mills went into receivership in 1906, victimized by poor management, outdated equipment, and dissatisfied labor, the hotel also began a long, slow slide. It passed through several owners before M. E. Manning bought it for three thousand dollars in 1929. He continued to operate it as a hotel until his death in 1932; his daughter, Kelly Braswell, then converted it into an apartment building and lived there until her death decades later. It sat empty for years before optimistic new owners bought it in the early 1980s, hoping to restore and reopen the hotel. Their efforts failed, and it was dismantled in 1982.

Springs and Spas

From the mid-1800s to the first decades of the twentieth century, Mississippi was dotted with "spas" and "springs" and health resorts of one form or another. Most were built around wells or artesian springs, all supposedly with medicinal value. The smallest were little more than roadside inns, but the largest were sprawling megaliths, often housing several hundred people at a time. They offered a respite from the heat and disease of Delta summers and a family retreat where businessmen and planters could safely leave their wives and children for weeks at a time.

Almost all of the old resort hotels are gone. Their attraction waned with the increasing mobility of Mississippians and with medical advances which cast doubt on the healing powers of the waters. Many burned, their isolation transformed from an advantage to certain doom when fire trucks could not reach them in time. Others were simply abandoned, vandalized, and eventually razed. A rare surviving example is Castalian Springs, just west of Durant, which still stands as a classic example of the two-story, wide-galleried spa hotel.

In the mid-1930s, Works Progress Administration writers traversed the state and recorded the last days of many of the dwindling resorts. Their descriptions rarely indicated that the days of the hotels were very numbered. Owens Wells, in Holmes County near Lexington, was described only as "a large rambling hotel . . . built near the wells and many people patronized it, especially the Delta people."[33] Stafford

OWENS

Stafford Inn (Stafford Springs)
Vossburg, Miss.

Lafayette Springs Hotel, ca. 1900. Photo courtesy of Patricia B. Young.

Springs, close to Laurel, was noted to be "one of the State's best known mineral springs. Before the coming of the white man, the Indians resorted here regularly to drink what they called bok-humma (Ind., red water). The rambling gray frame hotel (Open April through September) reflects the orange of the hills in its sloping roof."[34]

Brown's Wells, between Hazlehurst and Beauregard, was "a health and pleasure resort built around seven wells containing large quantities of minerals . . . [S]hortly after the [Civil] war a hotel and cottages were built to capitalize the wells' attractions. The resort is now a part of a 2200-acre tract on which are week-end cottages, a dancing pavilion, a swimming pool, and a nine-hole golf course."[35] Greenwood Springs was located in "a tiny village" in Itawamba County, with "an old-fashioned, latticed summer house enclosing the spring, the white frame hotel with rambling galleries, and the scattered village homes [with] a rustic simplicity representative of the Tennessee Hills."[36]

Some spas disappeared without a trace. Lafayette Springs still has a sign pointing north off Highway 6 between Oxford and Pontotoc, but the white frame hotel has vanished. Allison's Wells was once one of the most famous of Mississippi's spas, making a successful transition from health resort to artists' colony before burning in a January 1963 fire. *Madison County Herald* reporter Jim Lacey, Jr., followed the flames to Way, Mississippi, on that cold afternoon:

Previous page:
top: Owens Wells Hotel, ca. 1920. Photo courtesy of MDAH.
bottom: Stafford Springs Hotel, ca. 1910. Photo courtesy of MDAH.

> Allison's Wells, a rambling, old-time spa and art center 10 miles north of Canton, burned to the ground shortly after noon Monday, going up in a tremendous pillar of flame and smoke that only a big, old-frame building can cause. None of the paintings or other treasures in the hotel were saved. . . . By the time the Canton Fire Department arrived on the scene about 12:40, the building was engulfed in flames. Though the fire started in the center of the rambling building, it burned through the northern portion first because of the wind from the south. The last section to go was the Fishes' Club, so named because it held the dressing rooms and snack bar serving the swimmers in the nearby pool.[37]

An Episcopal conference center now stands on the site of Allison's Wells, the last traces of the resort and its outbuildings having been demolished years ago.

Lynne Castle

Pass Christian, from its earliest days, was a summer haven for rich and influential Louisianans, who considered it a pleasant outlying suburb of New Orleans. One of the most powerful of these two-state citizens was Lynne B. Watkins, a lawyer who earned a place on the Louisiana Supreme Court in the late 1800s. He purchased the rambling structures housing an Episcopal school in 1892 and moved his family to Pass Christian for the summer. It was soon apparent that the twenty-three rooms were more than he needed, and he converted the school into Lynne Castle.

Most of Pass Christian's hotels welcomed a wide clientele, including vacationing families, businessmen, and overnight guests. From the beginning, Lynne Castle was touted as being strictly a family resort, advertising that "transient trade is not catered to at all."[38] Its broad lawns stretched a hundred yards from the main building to Scenic Drive, and the hotel itself was "elegantly furnished and outfitted in every particular . . . a house of large airy rooms with halls and galleries well-heated and well-ventilated in the winter and cool and breezy in the summer."[39]

Guests could brave the gulf waters or, if they chose, bathe in a more controlled environment. A long wharf with bathing pavilions stretched several hundred yards into the water, but "[f]or those who are not in very good health and do not care to stand the cold plunge in the waters of the Gulf, there are hot and cold water bath rooms specially constructed in the house."[40]

Lynne Castle, ca. 1900. Photo courtesy of Pass Christian Historical Society (from the Bruce Stinson Collection).

Justice Watkins continued to spend his summers at Lynne Castle, along with dozens of families who made the hotel their yearly vacation destination. The resort stood on U.S. 90 at Henderson Avenue until 1917, when dry leaves piled on the kitchen's flat roof caught a spark. Within hours, the main building was lost. The site would be visited by tragedy once again, fifty-two years later, when Hurricane Camille blasted directly through the Richelieu Apartments, killing twenty-three of its residents.

Natchez Hotel

Natchez established Mississippi's tradition of elite hotels, dating back to the antebellum Parker's Hotel and Mansion House. These hostelries catered to the wealthy of the Cotton Kingdom and faded away as that prosperous era came to an end.

By the 1890s, Natchez was once again booming and competing with other towns in Mississippi for industry and new businesses. A group of local investors pooled $150,000 to erect an elegant five-story hotel on the corner of Franklin and Pearl

Natchez Hotel, ca. 1905.
Photo courtesy of MDAH.

Natchez Hotel, ca. 1920. Photo courtesy of the Thomas and Joan Gandy Collection.

streets. On September 1, 1891, the Natchez Hotel opened for business, touting its electric lights, elevators, telephones, and fine dining facilities. A balloon-like tower soared above the street-level stone archways. Looming over passersby were eerie cast-iron faces set into the brickwork.

For more than thirty years, the Natchez was the preferred hotel in the downtown area. A devastating fire in 1926 destroyed most of the building, but the owners refurbished the remaining rooms and continued to operate for another thirty years.

During the 1960s, the Natchez Hotel succumbed to competition from more modern motels and the need for downtown space. It was torn down to make way for a parking lot, erasing all but a few remnants of its heyday. The observant stroller on Franklin Street can still look up into those cast-iron visages peering down as the only evidence left of their elegant origins.

Carroll Hotel

Vicksburg in the 1890s was a booming river town, its miserable days of siege and deprivation rapidly fading memories. Money was plentiful, the wharves were packed with steamboats, and entrepreneurs were constantly looking for new ways to invest their wealth.

One of the most accomplished of those investors was Captain Edward C. Carroll, a self-made success from St. Louis who settled in Vicksburg after an early career on the Mississippi River. He dabbled in wharfboats, Yazoo River steamboats, banking, timber companies, a cotton press, oil mills, insurance, gas production, and elevators. But his most enduring contribution was as one of the 127 backers of a hotel in downtown Vicksburg, apparently with enough of his own ready cash to merit having it named for him.

The Carroll Hotel was completed in 1890 at a cost of $150,000. Perched on one of the precipitous hills leading down to the river, it was an impressive sight. "Driving up from the depot, for the first time, the stranger cannot fail to be struck with the metropolitan aspect of the hotel, towering above the buildings near by, and making the largest of them look diminutive by contrast. The clean looking ornamental front, faced with pressed brick of two colors, the first story mixed with gray sandstone, broken by projections which form towers, set off by numerous bay windows, the Carroll presents the appearance of a modern hotel, which in fact it is, both in beauty of exterior, and the perfections of its appointments."[41]

Along with ninety-two guest rooms, the Carroll offered ground-floor storefronts, billiard rooms, a grand rotunda, and an oak staircase. The passenger elevator "run by hydraulic pressure"[42] was a curious oddity in 1890. One hundred and fifty adults could be accommodated in the main dining room, with their children cared for in a separate facility. The ladies would have their own sitting room to use while the men would be entertained in the billiard hall.

Oddly enough, being far and away the most elegant of Vicksburg's hostelries, the Carroll struggled. Its completion was an anticlimax, as it remained empty for several months before stockholders relented to offer it rent-free for a year to "any reliable hotel man."[43] L. L. Mivilez of Arkansas finally took them up on their offer, but resigned in defeat after a year of less-than-optimal business. G. B. Duy took the reins in 1895; a promotional

Carroll Hotel, ca. 1895. Photo courtesy of Old Courthouse Museum, Vicksburg.

brochure of the day optimistically predicted that management of the Carroll would "afford him a well improved opportunity to demonstrate his ability as a host."[44]

Sometime during the 1900s, the Carroll was renamed the Jefferson Davis, but its fortunes continued to decline. A 1930s photo shows it still in business, with a fanciful iron canopy extending over the sidewalk along Walnut Street. Thirty years later, it was an empty shell, surrounded by plywood screens to protect passersby as its towers and bay windows were demolished.

White House Hotel

In 1895, Walter White filled the site of the old Garenflo Oyster Company, overlooking the Mississippi Sound at Biloxi, with tons of oysters shells. He built a large home there and went back to the law practice which would eventually elevate him to a posi-

White House Hotel, ca. 1930. Photo courtesy of James S. Love, III.

White House Hotel, ca. 1910. Photo courtesy of James S. Love, III.

tion as a circuit court judge. His wife, Cora, finding extra space in the Victorian mansion, rented out a few rooms to local schoolteachers. From that decision grew one of the coast's legendary hotels, the vaunted White House.

Mrs. White was an excellent hostess, and within a decade of her first rental foray, she had purchased her next-door-neighbor's house and become a full-time hotelier. The two houses were hooked together with a pillared front porch and balcony. The interior rooms were transformed into a large lobby and dining room. Live bands were a fixture of the White House, along with homegrown vegetables, milk straight from the Whites' own cows, and flowers from their hothouse.

As business boomed, Mrs. White bought up the whole block of seven mansions, then hooked on two Spanish Colonial annexes with private baths. Judge White returned from a trip to New England with plans to install a "color fountain" on the lawn, which would spew dancing columns of brightly hued water forty feet in the air. It became a Biloxi landmark and a source of entertainment for White House guests and local citizens.

Mrs. White died in 1934, having shepherded her simple idea of renting rooms to teachers into one of the Gulf Coast's most successful hotel empires. The White House was sold to James Love, Jr., owner of the nearby Buena Vista. He oversaw modernization of the original buildings and added a curved swimming pool.

The Love family sold the hotel in 1971, and it began a long decline. In 1988, bankruptcy was declared, and the now-decrepit old building was boarded up and forgotten. Ironically, it would be James Love III who would step forward to rescue the White House when it appeared to be beyond salvaging. A new White House is being built within the framework of the one-hundred-year-old hotel, lending a rare happy ending to the story of one of Mississippi's lost landmarks.

Great Southern Hotel

The most elusive dream in late-1800s Mississippi was the completion of a Jackson-to-Gulf Coast railroad line. First envisioned in the 1830s, the Gulf and Ship Island Railroad had sputtered and faltered repeatedly, defeating even the indomitable W. H. Hardy, founder of Hattiesburg. Hardy managed to complete a rail line from New Orleans to Meridian but finally despaired of completing tracks from the capital city to the beach.

Pennsylvania Civil War veteran Joseph T. Jones snapped up the bankrupt railroad in the 1890s, vowing not only to complete the line but to build a city to anchor it. He was true to his word, driving the last spike in 1896 and dredging a deep ship channel for the newly created port of Gulfport in 1899. At the height of the south Mississippi lumbering boom, Gulfport would be shipping more yellow pine than any other city in America.

Jones was determined to promote Gulfport not only as a shipping base but as a vacation mecca. To accommodate the crowds which he was certain would flock to the "Riviera of the South," he built the Great Southern Hotel in 1902–03. It opened to great fanfare in June 1903, luring guests in with the unheard-of luxuries of a telephone in each room and baths shared by only two rooms each. A promotional brochure from that year extolled the attributes of the Great Southern at length:

> They have built there as fine a tourist hotel as can be found anywhere in the South, if not in the world, and now it seems as though an army of men are at work building a city which is adequate to the hotel . . . The hotel is as charming in location and as perfect in appointment as any I ever visited . . . The hotel is appropriately named the 'Great Southern'. It is quite close to

Great Southern Hotel, ca. 1930. Photo courtesy of MDAH.

the water's edge, being only a few hundred yards distant and within sound of the gentle lapping of the surf upon the beach . . . It is a three-story frame building, as nearly fireproof as it is possible to make it of wood construction; has a frontage of 350 feet on the water, with two wings running back to the park in the rear, making a total frontage of about 600 feet. There are 250 rooms, every one of which is an outside room; there is a telephone in every room, also running hot and cold water, and there is a bath for every two rooms. The plumbing, by the way, is as fine as any I ever saw in our best metropolitan houses.

Special attention seems to have been given to the furnishings, which are in the best of taste and evidently selected with special reference to comfort and sanitation . . . The rotunda is finished in antique oak, the large dining room in Flemish oak. The latter, by the way, is charmingly situated on the ground floor, having two sides on the water . . . Another particularly enjoyable feature is the palm room, which is a favorite rendezvous for the guests of the house, both ladies and gentlemen . . . This is connected with the billiard room, which is patronized freely by both sexes; the box ball court in the same room providing mild and delightful exercise for all.[45]

Inn-by-the-Sea, ca. 1940. Photo courtesy of Pass Christian Historical Society (from the Bruce Stinson Collection).

The Great Southern was a city within itself. An 840-foot-deep artesian well pumped water into each room, and "a complete system of sewerage carries all waste 1/2 mile into the Gulf."[46] An independent power plant generated steam heat and electric power for the lights. An in-house orchestra played daily in the lobby and twice weekly for evening balls. Horses and buggies could be rented for shady rides to Pass Christian or Biloxi, and a trolley saved guests the long walk down the pier to the Gulfport Yacht Club's pavilion.

The hotel grew and thrived along with its new city. Southerners filled its rooms in summer, and winter migrants from Chicago could reach the beach by train in a mere twenty-six hours. But as the "Gold Coast" hotels of the 1920s rose, business slackened, and the Great Depression dealt the Great Southern a crippling blow. It closed briefly in the summer of 1933 but reopened in the fall of 1934, under the ownership of fifty-one Gulfport investors. Fading into a shadow of its former glory, it held on until the 1950s, when it was bulldozed to make way for downtown development.

Inn-by-the-Sea

Pass Christian's days as the "Saratoga of the South" were drawing to a close when Inn-by-the-Sea was built in 1920. The great beachfront hotels were deteriorating or already gone, victims of hurricanes, fire, and the gradual loss of the tourism business to Florida. Inn-by-the-Sea and the Pine Hills Hotel were last-ditch attempts to capitalize on the beauty and pastoral serenity of the Bay of St. Louis.

Inn-by-the-Sea was a fanciful Mediterranean castle nestled on seventy-five acres of Henderson Point. Its bell tower was a landmark overlooking private sand beaches, a nine-hole golf course, and tennis courts. Photos from the mid-1920s show sunbathers relaxing on the beaches and strolling along shaded terraces.

The stock market crash and Great Depression dealt a near-fatal blow to the Inn. It limped along through the 1930s and finally closed completely in 1942. The U.S. merchant marine added barracks and maintained it as a training facility for a number of years, but it had been empty and moldering for ages when it was demolished in July 1970. The site was converted for use as a Baptist conference center and campground.

Edgewater Gulf Hotel

Seventy years before the casino-and hotel building frenzy along Mississippi's Gulf Coast, another construction boom changed the skyline along Highway 90, then known as the Old Spanish Trail. From Bay St. Louis to Biloxi, a string of luxury hotels sprang up, each a bit more elegant and larger than its neighbor. All had their unique amenities, but none rivaled the Edgewater Gulf.

Designed by Chicago architect Benjamin Marsh, the Edgewater was an oasis set on six hundred acres of manicured lawns, gardens, and golf courses. Its two-million-dollar cost was astounding in 1924, and it quickly drew crowds both from Mississippi and

Edgewater Gulf Hotel, ca. 1950. Photo courtesy of MDAH.

neighboring states and from northern venues. An early promotional brochure painted an enticing portrait:

> Deep in the glamorous Old South, the Edgewater Gulf Hotel is a resort of unusual year-round appeal and distinction whether one is seeking quiet rest or active recreation. Wide shaded lawns sweep down to the Gulf of Mexico. Around the Hotel extend over 600 acres of our own beautiful estate-like grounds, extending to the Gulf on the south, and the Bay of Biloxi on the north. Through groves of venerable moss-hung oaks, magnolias and palmettos, winding hedge-bordered walks and rustic bridle paths beckon one to explore. . . . The Edgewater Gulf itself is a large, modern, fireproof structure, air conditioned designed for comfort and gracious living. Over 95% of the 400 delightful guest rooms command a glorious view of the azure Gulf. . . .[47]

A nine-hundred-foot deep well pumped 250,000 gallons of artesian water into the swimming pool daily, leading its owners to claim that a plunge into the pool would "perform wonders for children who are inclined to be of frail constitution."[48] Paying three dollars per day per person for a double room, guests could play eighteen holes of golf without ever leaving the grounds of the hotel.

Weathering the depression and following the lead of the Buena Vista into the post–World War II convention business, the Edgewater welcomed such famous guests as Harry Truman, Al Jolson, and Jeanette MacDonald. It began to lose ground in the 1960s, unsuccessfully struggling to compete with newer motels and the lure of Florida's more attractive beaches. A closing ceremony in May 1971 preceded the final locking of the doors. On a Sunday morning in July of that year, six hundred pounds of dynamite was wired into the walls, and Highway 90 was blocked to protect passing motorists from the impending demolition. An eyewitness reported the dawn scene: "There was a sound like low, rumbling thunder, then a tower of dust rose and blacked out the view of the great old Edgewater Gulf Hotel at Biloxi. But when the dust cleared most of the old hotel was still standing."[49] Two hundred fifty additional pounds of dynamite were added, and the towering hotel finally collapsed on Sunday afternoon, blocking traffic along the highway for miles in both directions. The rubble was swept away, and the coast's first enclosed shopping center rose on the site, memorializing the great hotel in its name, Edgewater Mall.

Buena Vista Hotel

On July 4, 1924, the doors to the Buena Vista Hotel in Biloxi were flung open, and a new era of Gulf Coast hospitality was ushered into existence. The four-hundred-thousand-dollar, five-story, two-hundred-room mission style stucco masterpiece was designed and built by noted architect Carl E. Matthes, who also designed the Tivoli Hotel just down the beach. The Buena Vista epitomized the wide-open lifestyle of the 1920s coast, bursting at the seams throughout the winter and summer months with sunseekers, gamblers, and high rollers.

The depression struck it a near-fatal blow. Mississippians had little spare money to spend on luxury during the Great Depression. Northerners who had once packed trains heading south for the winter kept their sweaters on and their wallets closed. When local attorney James S. Love, Jr., took a leap of faith and invested in the dying hotel in 1938, it was struggling for summer and winter guests and closed altogether through the spring and fall. Love pioneered the radical notion of courting convention business, giving people a reason to gather and spend money during the slow months. The first year, four groups trickled in for meetings. But within fifteen years, Love and the famously attentive Buena Vista staff had revolutionized Gulf Coast tourism, pulling in

Buena Vista Hotel, ca. 1950. Photo courtesy of James S. Love, III.

125 conventions of at least fifty people each and every year. The Hurricane Room was added, notable for its fifteen-hundred-guest seating capacity and the huge rear doors big enough to admit tractor-trailers.

The Buena Vista was on a roll. Each summer, the Miss Hospitality Pageant took over the convention rooms, and WLOX-TV broadcast live from its studio off the lobby. Bob Hope, Tom Mix, Frank Lloyd Wright, and Erle Stanley Gardner added their names to the guest register and their fame to the cachet of the hotel. In 1958, a modern hotel addition was added on the beach side of Highway 90 to accommodate the overflowing crowds.

Times were good for all the great beach hotels of the gulf, but change was on the horizon. Chain motels were drawing away family business, and the interstate highway was nearing completion north of Biloxi and Gulfport. The Gulf Coast Coliseum lured away more and more convention business and eventually snagged the Miss Hospitality Pageant as well. As the outlook for the Buena Vista dimmed, nature added insult to injury. Hurricane Camille blasted through the windows of the grand old hotel, where WLOX broadcasters valiantly stayed on the air until water rose above their

Buena Vista Hotel Lobby, ca. 1950. Photo courtesy of James S. Love, III.

Buena Vista Hotel, ca. 1960. Photo courtesy of James S. Love, III.

equipment. The aftermath of the storm revealed a ruined lobby and grounds littered with snapped trees and debris from all along the beach.

James Love sold the property in 1971. Through a series of owners, it gradually sagged and deteriorated. Within ten years, the lack of business was evident in the peeling plaster, stained carpets, and littered hallways. The beach motel unit became the primary wing, and only when it was full were guests routed across to the main building. The doors were locked altogether during fall and early winter as an energy-saving measure. Plans to route a loop of I-110 right past the hotel kept developers away, despite suggestions of use as a senior citizens' center, children's hospital, or condominiums.

An arsonist destroyed any hope of reviving the shell of the Buena Vista in 1991. Most of the west and central wings were consumed, and the empty hulk was vandalized and stripped of all salvageable materials. The Biloxi Belle Casino purchased the ruins in 1993 and demolished what was left of the Buena Vista for a casino parking garage.

Pine Hills Hotel

In the years before the Civil War, William Whitfield cleared the cypress swamps on the north shore of the Bay of St. Louis to build Shelly Plantation. It was nine miles from the Pass Christian Hotel, the harbinger of the resort trade that would transform this end of the Gulf Coast.

By the 1920s, Whitfield was long dead, and the old Shelly Plantation had reverted to wilderness. New Orleans architect Moise Goldstein, the designer of the Audubon Zoo, was hired in the middle of that decade to build a grand luxury hotel on the site, the first of the renowned Gulf Coast hostelries which would earn the stretch from Bay St. Louis to Biloxi the nickname "Gold Coast."

The site was a natural. Just a stone's throw off the Old Spanish Trail Highway, one of America's first transcontinental roadways, its twenty-three hundred acres included three and a half miles of shoreline along the Bay of St. Louis. The road from Spanish Trail wound through a mile and a half of knobby cypress trees. The swamps were once again drained and log roads built to support the heavy machinery lumbering in to work on the great hotel. A December 1926 newspaper article captured the community's fascination with the towering structure rising across the bay:

> Everyone who has viewed Pine Hills Hotel is most enthusiastic over the really magnificent building and its more than usually beautiful furnishings. The stockholders who viewed the building at the reception and inspection Saturday night believe that they have achieved by the shores of Bay St. Louis one of the finest resort hotels in the country. Great numbers of Coast people from Mobile to New Orleans and all points between motored to the hotel yesterday and many viewed the hotel. Hal Thompson, president of the hotel company and manager of the hotel, stated this morning that the hotel is open to the public for inspection and the visitors are heartily welcome, that there are guides present at all times to conduct visitors through the building, and that the hotel people desire the people of the Coast, tourists and visitors from all parts of the country to view this exceptionally fine hotel.[50]

The Pine Hills Hotel opened with a gala celebration on December 18, 1926. Mississippi's Lieutenant Governor Dennis Murphree joined hundreds of guests in the Spanish lounge and grand lobby to open "The Jewel of the Gulf." It was an instant success. Every one of its 185 rooms, each with private bath, was booked through the end of February 1927. Guests would arrive by yacht from the Pass Christian train station, or would drive their Model T's and Merry Oldsmobiles down the tree-lined drive from the highway, passing the eighteen-hole golf course and luxury residential lots. They could park in the three-story circular parking garage, the first built in America. Once checked in at the Pine Hills, they would enjoy not only the ornate Spanish Lounge, but also an opulent dining room, a recreation hall, and convention rooms. On the grounds, their time was split between the fishing pier, yacht marina, tennis courts, and rounds of golf, followed by food and drink at the seventy-five-thousand-dollar clubhouse. An in-house orchestra filled the formal rooms with music during dinner and dancing.

As the Roaring Twenties peaked, the New Orleans investors who built Pine Hills were reveling in the rewards of their creation. They shrugged off concerns about construction of the new Highway 90 bridge, visible in the distance as it marched slowly across the mouth of the bay. Certainly, when it opened, fewer cars would be turning off the Old Spanish Trail to Pine Hills. But business was brisk, and the five-story "Pink Palace" filled its rooms most nights. The owners saw nothing but success in their future.

The euphoria was short-lived. In October 1929, the hotel was packed, and staff members scurried about, decorating the Spanish Lounge for a Halloween ball. In the basement, vacationing businessmen smoked cigars and watched the ticker tape machine churning out results from the New York Stock Exchange. The markets were

Pine Hills Hotel, ca. 1926. Photo courtesy of MDAH.

tumbling, and their fall would carry the Pine Hills with it. As the tape's news worsened, frantic guests threw clothes in their suitcases, checked out, and hurried home to Chicago and St. Louis. The Halloween ball was forgotten, and the hotel, for the first time, echoed with the emptiness that would come to be its signature.

Within weeks, two of the three banks holding notes on Pine Hills had foreclosed. Business had vanished in the wake of America's slide into economic chaos. By the end of November 1929, less than three years after its grand opening, the great hotel was closed. It would never function as a resort again. From 1929 until 1942, a lone caretaker lived in the empty hulk. The U.S. Army leased it for six months in 1942 as a barracks. A 1947 hurricane battered the shell, which held against the wind and water. The golf courses disappeared under unmowed grass. Residential lots, once touted as Mississippi's premier neighborhood, sheltered nothing but snakes and weeds.

From 1952 until 1968, the Catholic Oblate Fathers occupied the sprawling hotel, converting it into Our Lady of the Snows Scholasticate, with fifty-nine students. The dining room was transformed into a library and the Spanish Lounge into a chapel. Then the priests moved on. In August 1969, as Gulf Coast residents frantically nailed up plywood and watched the skies blacken with the approach of Hurricane Camille,

Pine Hills sat empty and unprotected. The massive storm blew right past the forty-three-year-old hotel, barely damaging the concrete and hollow tile structure. Over the next ten years, occasional schemes to turn it into condominiums or a luxury resort surfaced and just as quickly evaporated.

Du Pont Chemical Corporation bought the property in 1984 to buffer its industrial acreage in DeLisle. Despite valiant efforts of a local preservation group, the long-forgotten hotel was demolished in November 1986. Demolition teams found their wrecking balls and battering rams to be all but useless against the solidly built behemoth, and the hotel was finally dismantled by hand. Nothing remains but a pier and an overgrown driveway, the few foundation remnants hidden beneath weeds and underbrush.

Chapter Three

Churches and Synagogues

MISSISSIPPI'S RELIGIOUS TRADITION is manifested in the architectural diversity of its churches, ranging from tiny clapboard rural sanctuaries to towering cathedrals and multistructured ecclesiastical campuses. The state is the undisputed "buckle" of the "Bible Belt," but the oft-forgotten fact is that religion was slow to take hold and almost universally disorganized until decades after the formation of the Mississippi Territory.

French missionaries were the first to venture down the Mississippi River from Canada and introduce European religion to the Natchez Indians. D'Iberville's sailors had scarcely made landfall on the Gulf Coast before Mass was observed. The earliest permanent settlers who came to make a home in Mississippi were Protestant Englishmen, and they were joined by Catholic Spaniards in 1781.

Relations between the English settlers and the Spaniards were generally congenial through the 1790s. Though Catholicism was the official state religion during the period of Spanish rule, Protestants were tolerated as long as they kept a low profile. A small group of Baptists met in Mary Stampley's home at Coles Creek in 1791, banding together to start a formal church. Trouble flared when Pastor Richard Curtis defied Spanish authorities by performing a Protestant wedding ceremony. Threatened with arrest and deportation to the salt mines, he fled the area, returning only after American rule took effect in 1798.

St. Paul's Catholic Church *(See page 98.)*

Residents of the old Atlantic states were eyeing the new Mississippi territory for its land and natural resources, but also for its unchurched souls. In 1799, the South Carolina Conference of the Methodist Church sent Reverend Tobias Gibson to scout out the ecclesiastical leanings of the people in southwest Mississippi. He found enough interest to start a small congregation at Washington and had added eight other "churches" to his "circuit" within a year. The Presbyterians weren't far behind; in 1800, the Carolina Presbytery sent three missionaries into the Natchez District to plant nine "preaching stations." Baptists, as always, were a more loosely organized lot. Local groups formed, and by 1806 there were six established churches in the Mississippi Association.

These early efforts were valiant but ignored by most territorial-era Mississippians. Despite the efforts of such renowned clergymen as Lorenzo Dow, who hired slave boys to hide in trees and shriek during his doomsday sermons, fewer than 5 percent of Mississippians were professed churchgoers in 1817. Some of this lack of participation was due to the isolated nature of homesteads and lack of opportunity. But even in cosmopolitan Natchez, the arrival of statehood found fewer than one in five Natchezians in church on Sunday morning. A visitor to Natchez noted that the citizens of that city were more preoccupied with worldly matters. "All make love; most of them play; and a few make money. With Religion they have nothing to do."[1] Lorenzo Dow lamented, "I find it almost impossible to get the people out to meeting any way, and had my scruples whether there were three Christians in town, either black or white."[2] Times were so desperate for the few Catholic faithful that their unused church was rented out as a public hall at the odd rate of one peppercorn per year.

As the state filled with settlers in the 1820s and 1830s, religion took a somewhat firmer hold. Many of the new landowners had come from established communities along the East Coast, and they were determined to bring their religious traditions with them. Money was increasingly plentiful, and churches could be built. In the "cities" such as Natchez and Vicksburg, these churches often reflected the prosperity of the early Cotton Kingdom. A group of wealthy aristocrats met at palatial Auburn to plan the formation of Trinity Episcopal Church in 1823, goaded into action by the impending marriage of one of their children and the lack of appropriate space for such an event. Trinity Episcopal rose with brick pillars and a towering cupola.

Most antebellum churches were much more modest. The decade of the 1840s was the era of church building in Mississippi; the 1860 census showed a total of 1,441 religious buildings extant, 75 percent of which had been built in the 1840s. Most were similar to the Presbyterian church in rural Kemper County: "A log cabin open to the roof, dirt floor, benches of split logs, pulpit of clapboards perched halfway up to the end of the wall, stick and dirt chimney, two doors with board shutters, and, for windows, cracks between the logs."[3] Sometimes more ambitious structures were flashy on the outside and empty on the inside. St. Mary's Cathedral in Natchez was begun in 1842 with high hopes and a two-hundred-foot spire soaring above the Gothic facade, at a cost of forty thousand dollars. Unfortunately, that was as far as the congregation could go; for almost twenty years, it sat as an incomplete shell with unplastered interior walls and temporary pews.

As church attendance grew, formal organizations developed. By 1846, there were eleven thousand Methodists enrolled in churches. The Baptists claimed four hundred churches with over twenty-one thousand members. The Catholics had grown to have eleven churches and as many priests, overseeing six hundred members in churches along the Mississippi River, Gulf Coast, and in central Mississippi. Presbyterians and Episcopalians tended to be clustered in the more established towns and attracted a wealthier, better-educated congregation than the Methodists or Baptists. Commenting on the Episcopal Church's thirty-three parishes and 940 communicants, Joseph Holt Ingraham took note of the "opulent planters, merchants and professional men."[4]

Jewish migration into Mississippi had begun during territorial days, when persecution drove them from Germany and Alsace-Lorraine. Its antebellum peak in the 1840s brought enough Jewish people together in towns like Natchez, Vicksburg, Woodville, and Jackson to form loose congregations, although their building programs were generally delayed until the post–Civil War era.

Sectional differences, mainly over slavery, had led the state's Baptists and Methodists to break from their national organizations in the 1840s. The Southern Baptist denomination and Methodist Episcopal Church South were strongly in favor of continued slavery, and many of their church balconies were filled on Sunday morning with black members. The Episcopal and Presbyterian churches maintained ties with their national organizations, but on any given Sunday in the 1850s, many preachers in Mississippi were likely to be extolling the positive aspects of slavery and the need for eventual secession.

When secession did come for Mississippi, it affected a populace that had managed to find religion over the previous forty years. One-third of those listed in the 1860 census claimed a church affiliation of some sort, three-quarters of those either Methodist or Baptist. War and Reconstruction took a toll on the religious edifices just as on secular buildings, with many churches abandoned or burned. When they were rebuilt, black members went their own way and built their own sanctuaries. By 1890, the Negro Baptist churches alone numbered 1,385, with more than 136,000 members.

As the twentieth century began, church life was central to the social whirl in most Mississippi communities, and members were active in a number of social reforms. A 1906 survey found 657,000 church members among Mississippi's population of 1.7 million people. Baptists and Methodists, as always, claimed the majority. They were followed by the Catholics, Presbyterians, and Episcopalians and a surprisingly large number of Jewish congregations. There were seventeen temple groups ministering to 746 families throughout the state.

The first two decades of the century witnessed a building boom among churches, fueled by Mississippi's fast-growing cities and a need to replace the small frame structures of the post–Civil War era. Coinciding with the rise of neoclassicism, the era produced towering church facades with columns and steeples and silver domes. Less common but equally impressive were Gothic chapels and Romanesque structures.

Many still stand, although altered for modern worship trends. Others, such as Greenwood's First Baptist, Oxford's Cumberland Presbyterian, and Columbus's Christian Church were demolished in the name of progress. Nature destroyed others, including St. John's Episcopal in Glen Allan and St. Paul's Catholic Church in Vicksburg. Possibly the most tragic losses have been the elaborate Jewish synagogues, abandoned as their congregations dwindled and vanished.

St. John's Episcopal Church, Glen Allan

The antebellum Delta was a wild and forbidding place, largely unsettled until levees were built to hold back the annual floods and swamps drained to provide arable planting lands. Scattered villages and plantations appeared in the years preceding the Civil War, but the only settlement to rival those in southwest Mississippi was in Washington County. Along the shores of Lake Washington, just a stone's throw east of the Mississippi River, an intrepid band of Kentuckians cleared plantations in the 1820s. A few years later, they were joined by Carolinians on the south banks of the lake. They soon found that this hard-won land they had claimed grew cotton at a prodigious rate, and their architecture reflected their consequent prosperity. Belmont, Mount Holly, and Everhope were just a few of the legendary mansions built in the Glen Allan area. Planters with less foresight or more faith in nature built too close to the river's edge and lost their homes to the shifting Mississippi's currents.

St. John's Episcopal Church, ca. 1900. Photo courtesy of MDAH.

In 1848, the Episcopal Diocese of Mississippi admitted the Glen Allan congregation of St. John's to their union. Jonathon McCaleb donated several acres of Greenfield Plantation for the site on the east shore of Lake Washington. Construction with bricks burned on the site and native timber began in 1854. The church was finished and consecrated in April 1857, as described by Bishop William Mercer Green in his diary: "On April 5, 1857, their beatiful new church was consecrated under the name of St. John's."[5] He failed to note that a freak spring snowstorm shortened the service.

As the only organized church in the neighborhood, St. John's enjoyed almost universal community support. Mrs. P. E. Metcalfe described the camaraderie to the Washington County Historical Society: "A beautiful church was built on this land, handsomely furnished, and the whole neighborhood came to worship there as they seemed to have been all of one faith—Protestant Episcopal—at that time. This seems to have been the earliest Episcopal Church that was built in this part of the country."[6]

St. John's Episcopal Church Ruins, ca. 2000. Photo courtesy of Mary Rose Carter.

The church's first few years were successful, with new communicants joining under the leadership of Reverend Amos G. Treadway, a native New Yorker. The Civil War sent him fleeing home, took many of the church's supporters away to battle, and spelled doom for the young church. The leaded windows were taken out and the lead melted down for Confederate bullets, leaving the interior exposed to the harsh weather of the Delta. The little chapel sagged. Bishop Green decreed the building unfit for worship in 1869, and he was disturbed at the sight on his return visit in 1882: "I rode to the church and found it a ruin indeed, though a beautiful one. . . ."[7]

St. John's sat empty for another twenty years, quiet and forlorn as vines crept in through the empty windows. In 1900, a new generation of Deltonians was enjoying prosperity and making plans to refurbish the old church. A spring tornado ended those dreams. Walls and roof weakened from a half-century of exposure crumbled in the whirlwind, leaving only a skeletal remnant looming over the graveyard.

Cumberland Presbyterian Church

In an August 1864 photo of Oxford's square, an imposing Greek Revival church is seen in the upper lefthand corner. Its temple-form facade is fronted by six Tuscan columns. If the image is the Cumberland Presbyterian Church, one of the few structures to survive Federal destruction of Oxford, then its form was drastically altered in later years. The sanctuary that was torn down in the 1940s was an equally impressive Gothic structure with elaborate stonework and arched windows. Its demolition aroused emotions nearly as volatile as those that had brought destruction to the square eighty years before.

The Cumberland Presbyterians set up in Oxford around 1837, building a log sanctuary on the east side of the square. Their numbers multiplied so rapidly that an Oxford matron complained that "the Cumberlands and the dog fennel are about to take the town."[8] A brick church was later built, lost in an 1840s fire and replaced with their final church just south of the courthouse square. Notwithstanding the 1864 photograph, the most enduring Cumberland Presbyterian Church was a riot of multipatterned brickwork, tall lancet-shaped windows, and an unusual panelled set of front doors. It loomed over the simpler storefronts along South Lamar.

When the congregation dwindled in the twentieth century, Cumberland Presbyterian was razed for commercial development. William Faulkner lamented the loss in an angry letter to the *Oxford Eagle* when similar action threatened the Lafayette County Courthouse: "Bravo your piece about the preservation of the courthouse. I am afraid your cause is already lost though . . . [A]ll we have left now to distinguish an old southern town from any one of ten thousand towns built yesterday from Kansas to California are the Confederate monument, the courthouse and the jail . . . Your cause is doomed. They will go the way of the old Cumberland church. It was here in 1861; it was the only building on or near the square still standing in 1865. It was tougher than war, tougher than Yankee Brigadier Chalmers and his artillery and all his sappers with

Cumberland Presbyterian Church, ca. 1900. Photo courtesy of Patricia B. Young.

Cumberland Presbyterian Church, ca. 1900. Photo courtesy of Patricia B. Young.

First Baptist Church, Columbus, ca. 1900. Photo courtesy of MDAH.

dynamite and crowbars and cans of kerosene. But it wasn't tougher than the ringing of a cash register bell. It had to go—obliterated, effaced, no trace left—so that a sprawling octopus covering the country from Portland, Maine to Oregon can dispense in cut-rate bargain lots, bananas and toilet paper. They call this progress. But they don't say where it's going; also there are some of us who would like the chance to say whether or not we want the ride."[9]

First Baptist Church of Columbus

Columbus is a city noted for its remarkable antebellum domestic architecture, epitomized by the townhouses built by local planters. One of those planters was Major Thomas G. Blewett, a South Carolina native who migrated to Columbus in 1835. Major Blewett took over an entire block of downtown for his estate, crowding out the Masonic Lodge and St. Paul's Episcopal Church. He was philanthropic as well as successful, using his own funds to construct a bridge across the Luxapalilla River and giving eighteen thousand dollars to finance building of the original First Baptist Church.

In a time when most congregations in Mississippi were still meeting in homes or crude frame churches, First Baptist Church of Columbus was rising in the elaborate style of St. Michael's in Charleston, South Carolina. It was completed by 1840, a well-proportioned temple-form structure with four fluted Ionic columns supporting a full entablature and pediment. Tall, thin windows were capped with stone lintels. The most impressive feature, rising 115 feet over the young town of Columbus, was a five-stage octagonal steeple. An early member marvelled at the beauty of the church: "At the time of its completion it was the largest and handsomest church edifice in Mississippi, if not the entire South."[10]

First Baptist opened its doors as a hospital following the Battle of Shiloh. The fine carpets were ripped up and cut into squares for blankets. Columbus was never occupied by Union forces and escaped the physical damage wreaked on Corinth, Holly Springs, Jackson, and Vicksburg. Following the war, First Baptist replaced the carpet, and life went on. Its six hundred seats served its congregation well until 1908, when it was demolished, over the protests of many church members. Ten years later, a New York writer commented on the old and the new: "I have seen photographs of an old Baptist Church with a fine (and not at all Baptist-looking) portico and fluted columns, which was torn down to make room for the present stupidly commonplace Baptist Church."[11]

First Christian Church of Columbus

For the first two years of the Civil War, Mississippi's government proceeded at its normal pace in its accustomed location, with most of its business conducted in the two blocks bounded by the Old Capitol and the Governor's Mansion. War had certainly affected the emphasis of legislation, but battles in Virginia and Tennessee, or even in Holly Springs and Corinth, had little effect on the capital city.

All that changed with General Grant's push toward Vicksburg. Jackson was occupied by Union troops in May 1863 and once again following General Pemberton's surrender at Vicksburg. Governor Pettus and his staff loaded up what government papers they could, along with most of the Governor's Mansion furniture, and fled east. Fifty years later, an official state publication commented on the tenor of the times: "During this troublesome period the Old State Capitol of Mississippi was the rendezvous of the

First Christian Church, Columbus, ca. 1900. Photo courtesy of MDAH.

rowdy military, and its records lay like soiled heaps of snow in its corridors and rotunders [*sic*]. It is true that the official government, which throughout the Confederacy had been tossed from pillar to post, in something of the manner of the English court at the time of Edward I, carried a portion of its archives in its train, and during these years the records were removed from the State House by Governors Pettus and Clark, in turn, and stored in no less than a dozen places, including Columbus, Enterprise, Meridian and Macon."[12] The first temporary capital was Meridian, but it quickly caught General Sherman's eye and was torched. The governor's retinue bounced down to Enterprise and then north to Columbus.

Fall of 1863 found Columbus serving as Mississippi's surrogate capital. The remnants of the legislature gathered there in November, the house of representatives claiming space in the Christian Church and the senate occupying the Lowndes County Courthouse, where newly elected Governor Charles Clark was inaugurated. Within a month, he was forced to move on to Macon, trailing the crumbling trappings of Mississippi's state sovereignty.

The Christian Church had seen its only days of notoriety. It survived another century before demolition.

St. Paul's Catholic Church, ca. 1890. Photo courtesy of Old Courthouse Museum, Vicksburg.

St. Paul's Catholic Church

Reverend John B. Bannon was a Missouri clergyman who gained renown for following Confederate troops onto the most hostile battlefields, comforting the wounded and dying and administering last rites under fire from Union gunners. General Sterling Price would later remember him as "the greatest soldier I ever saw . . . In the midst of the fray he would step in and take up a fallen soldier. If he were a Catholic, he would give him the rites of the Church; if a Protestant, and if he so desired, he would baptize him."[13]

Father Bannon followed his troops to Grand Gulf and into the besieged city of Vicksburg in the spring of 1863. He probably felt relatively safe in the sanctuary of the 1849 Gothic St. Paul's Catholic Church, with its solid brick walls, soaring arches, and boxed steeple. Unfortunately, the height of that steeple made the church a target for Union gunners. As Father Bannon said Mass on the morning of June 28, 1863, a 132-pound Parrott shell burst through one of St. Paul's arched windows, sailed across the pews, and crashed out another window, thumping harmlessly to the sidewalk. A soldier at the service recorded in his diary that, while no one was injured, the incident "badly freightened [*sic*] the women, who all left." He went on to say that "I had just gotten inside the door [when a shell] struck the railing outside the church, taking off the arm of a citizen who was coming in."[14] Father Bannon preached on, unfazed.

St. Paul's survived the siege and war, but was destroyed by another blow in 1953. A deadly December tornado left the church in shambles. The remains were razed soon after and the church rebuilt on the same site.

Anshe Chesed Temple

From its earliest days, Vicksburg was a magnet for Jewish immigrants. Between 1820 and 1840, an estimated twenty-five to thirty families settled there, with most opening mercantile stores. They worshipped in private homes with an occasional visiting rabbi. By 1841, there was enough support to formally incorporate the Hebrew Benevolent Congregation of the Men of Mercy.

Anshe Chesed Temple, ca. 1900. Photo courtesy of Old Courthouse Museum, Vicksburg.

Anshe Chesed Temple, ca. 1960. Photo courtesy of Old Courthouse Museum, Vicksburg.

Anshe Chesed Congregation was formed in 1862, just before Vicksburg and its Jewish community were dealt the crippling blow of siege and warfare. Along with their Christian neighbors, the congregation struggled back during Reconstruction. Their membership was increasing, and the time had come for a permanent temple. Twenty-five thousand dollars was raised through the sale of pews and private donations. A new brick Gothic-style synagogue on Cherry Street was dedicated in May 1870, with the whole city turning out to celebrate. Governor James L. Alcorn spoke from the pulpit, and the Vicksburg newspaper noted that "the interior of the Church presents a beautiful appearance and is not surpassed, if equaled by any Church in the city in point of workmanship."[15]

Eight years later, yellow fever swept into Vicksburg, claiming forty-six members of the Anshe Chesed congregation, including Rabbi Gotthelf. When the scourge finally ended, the temple members forged ahead, providing leadership in all phases of Vicksburg life. They altered their synagogue in 1893, transforming the Gothic facade into a more fashionable Romanesque design.

By 1900, Anshe Chesed included more than five hundred members, led by Rabbi Solomon, the "bicycling rabbi." He shunned the newfangled cars appearing on the hills of Vicksburg, preferring to use his two-wheeler to commute between home, the synagogue, and the private school he founded.

As in many other Mississippi towns, the later years of the twentieth century saw a dwindling Jewish population in Vicksburg. Older temple members died, their children moved on to larger cities, and gradually the temple fell into disrepair. It was damaged in the 1953 tornado, which claimed several members of the congregation. The old sanctuary was unair-conditioned, and parking was almost nonexistent. In the 1970s, a new temple was built near the Jewish cemetery. The old building was loaned to various congregations and sold to a painting contractor. The steeple was known to be termite-ridden and unstable, and plaster peeled from interior walls. After several attempts at alternative use or rehabilitation, the owner had the temple demolished in 1982.

Temple Beth Israel, Jackson

The first home of the Beth Israel congregation in Jackson was a frame structure on South State Street, built in 1861 and destroyed by fire during the Federal occupation of Jackson in 1863. Eleven years later, it was replaced with a striking two-story brick-

Temple Beth Israel, Jackson, ca. 1900. Photo courtesy of MDAH.

and-stone building on the same site. That temple lasted only a year before an accidental fire destroyed it.

The third temple was more enduring, standing on the South State Street site from 1875 until it was dismantled in 1940. The dedication in June 1875 was a citywide affair, complete with a parade and elaborate ceremony. "The procession was formed in front of the City Hall . . . up President to Capitol, on Capitol to State and down State to the Temple, which was found to be already so crowded that many were unable to gain admission. It is a beautiful gothic building fifty-four feet in length by thirty-four in width and two stories high." The dedication was followed by a dusk-to-dawn ball at "Angelo's Hall."[16]

Beth Israel was a Gothic-style stone building with lancet-arched windows and twin curving stairs leading to the second-story sanctuary. Later photos show that these twin stairs were replaced with one broad stone stairway. When it was razed in 1940, it was

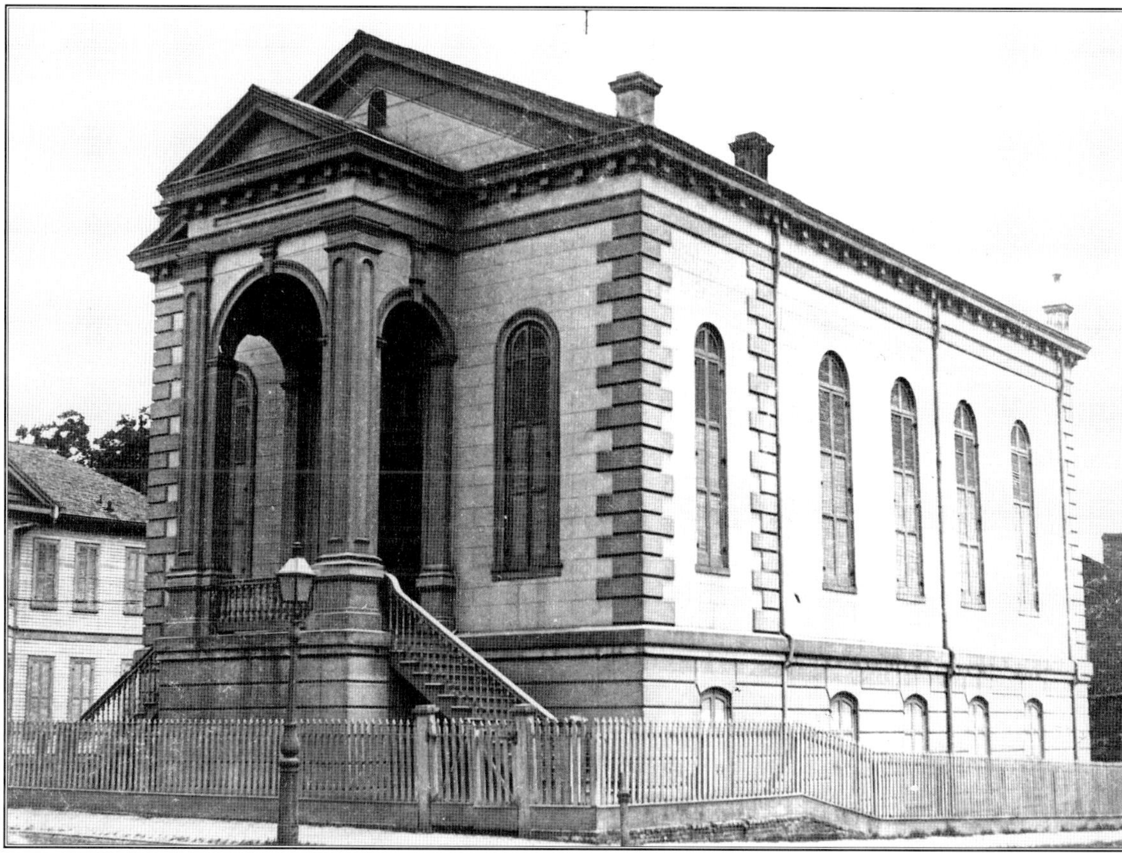

Temple B'nai Israel, ca. 1880. Photo courtesy of the Thomas and Joan Gandy Collection.

the oldest functioning religious building in Jackson. The congregation moved that year to more modern facilities on Woodrow Wilson Avenue and later to Old Canton Road.

Temple B'nai Israel

The Jewish community in Natchez dates its first members back to territorial days, but it truly grew into a congregation with the influx of French and German immigrants during the 1840s. Most came as peddlers, but were soon established merchants along the streets of Natchez Under the Hill and the more fashionable addresses along Main and Franklin streets.

Congregation B'nai Israel met in homes, businesses, and even the fire station before the Civil War. Although Natchez surrendered with minimal conflict, the one civilian casualty devastated the small Jewish congregation. Seven-year-old Rosalie Beekman, daughter of an Under-the-Hill merchant and a member of B'nai Israel, was caught in the crossfire when the Union gunboat *Essex* fired on Silver Street.

By 1867, the fifty Jewish families of Natchez had purchased a lot at the corner of Washington and Commerce for a temple. Their fund-raising efforts, including a masked ball, raffles, and other events, involved the entire community. The congregation met in the Baptist Church during temple construction. Young Clara Lowenberg described the excitement of working for the temple: "All the summer of my sixth year, the whole family was much interested in raising money to build a Temple . . . They gave a grand masked ball and everybody gave something to raffle or sell. Bishop Elder, a much admired Catholic Bishop gave a black marble paper weight, with an inlaid picture of St. Peters at Rome, my first introduction to desire to see foreign places . . . When the Temple was finally finished, there was great religious enthusiasm . . . Such a big crowd was expected that no children under seven could go! But I was such a religious little girl that had been so interested in the Temple that grandma took me . . ."[17]

B'nai Israel Temple served the Jewish community in Natchez for thirty-one years. Faulty wiring led to a November 1903 fire which totally destroyed the building. Two years later, the present temple was built on the same site.

Temple Beth Israel, Woodville

Woodville in the late 1800s was known as "Little Jerusalem." It was a fitting nickname for a community so ecumenically diverse that many of its businesses closed on Saturday morning so Christian merchants could attend Rabbi Cohen's services. Oddly enough, by the second decade of the twentieth century, the Jewish population had dwindled to almost nothing, and Temple Beth Israel was converted to a school.

The booming southwest corner of Mississippi attracted a vast number of European Jewish immigrants in the mid-1800s. Many settled in Natchez, but almost as many made their way downriver to Woodville, the thriving home of the West Feliciana Railroad. The Woodville Hebrew Educational Association was formed in the years following the Civil War, and from this group grew the Beth Israel congregation. They built their first Woodville synagogue in 1878, only to lose it to fire eighteen

Temple Beth Israel, Woodville, ca. 1900. Photo courtesy of MDAH.

years later. A new temple soon replaced it. Photos of that structure show an exuberant frame building with corner towers, inlaid woodwork, and a carved Torah in the pediment.

Death and migration of the younger members to cities decimated the Jewish population in Woodville, leaving no one to maintain the temple. In 1910, the building was sold to the American Legion, its pews and pulpit given to the neighboring Woodville Baptist Church. It was later moved several blocks and converted into a movie theatre. It burned sometime around 1930.

First Methodist Church of Ripley

Many of the Protestant congregations which now claim to be "First Baptist" or "First Methodist" or "First Presbyterian" of their community began as tiny groups of worshippers in someone's home. Their original buildings were often log or clapboard,

First Methodist Church, Ripley, ca. 1910. Photo courtesy of Ripley Public Library.

without ornamentation or frills. These church houses were replaced as the congregations enlarged and prospered.

One of the finest examples of nineteenth-century ecclesiastical architecture in Mississippi was First Methodist Church of Ripley. Reverend Charles Peter Miller was a circuit rider, born in 1798, who made his way to north Mississippi with his family. Shortly before his death in 1875, he described his career: "I removed with my wife and five children and arrived here the 24th day of July, 1836, before there was any town; put up a tent and built a house. The lots had been laid out but had not been sold. I found a few Methodists here and as soon as I built a cabin I organized a class of 26 members in the month of September, 1836. This place at that time was not in any circuit, but the same fall was included in the Salem Circuit. . . . I continued to preach as a local preacher from the time I was licensed up to the late Civil War. The church organization was broken up, and I was much encumbered in trying to take care of my property and to save it, and during the turmoil of four or five years of war and the entire disorganization of the church, I had lost much ground on the subject of sermonizing. . . . I look forward with confidence to be taken from the church militant to the church triumphant; I desire that the Church and the Masons give me a modest burial, not to be too hurried."[18]

Reverend Miller oversaw the erection of First Methodist's first sanctuary, built in 1850, and probably witnessed its burning by Federal troops in 1864. General A. J. Smith had ordered his troops to spare the town's houses of worship, but the Confederate hay stored in the Methodist church must have been too tempting a target. That church was replaced with another frame building, also lost to fire in 1886. In its place was built the clapboard Gothic structure with lancet windows and a tall, graduated steeple. It would serve First Methodist's congregation for forty years, finally being demolished after its steeple was destroyed in a storm.

Church of the Redeemer

In 1854, the Episcopal bishop of Mississippi formally consecrated the Church of the Redeemer in Biloxi as the coast's first Episcopal parish. This was a symbolic beginning for a Protestant denomination in a Catholic-dominated region, but the Church of the Redeemer would come to be a much more powerful symbol of memory and redemption in its next 150 years.

The church's first building was a simple frame structure at Howard and Nixon streets, completed in the 1850s. It was here that Jefferson Davis worshipped in his last years. His health deteriorating and his finances uncertain, he had moved into a friend's house at Beauvoir. As the Civil War was gradually transformed in southern minds from an ignominious defeat to a glorious Lost Cause, the Confederacy's only president was increasingly revered, even more so after his death. His pew in the Church of the Redeemer was marked with a silver plaque and a silk Confederate flag.

Church of the Redeemer, ca. 1940. Photo courtesy of MDAH.

Church of the Redeemer, ca. 1940. Photo courtesy of MDAH.

In 1891, a wealthy benefactor gave land for a new brick church on the beach road. Davis's wooden pew was moved into the new sanctuary and marked with a silver nameplate. The old church was deconsecrated and moved to the new site as a parish house. A steady stream of old soldiers and generals made the pilgrimage to the coast to visit their hero's church and read the framed letter in the vestibule, written by Davis to Reverend Hinsdale: "Enclosed I send a contribution, a small sum which you must regard not as the measure of my will, but of my ability. To you is made the confession that circumstances have made me poorer than an average fisherman, but other demands are here subordinate to the cause of Him who died for the redemption of fallen man."[19] In the sanctuary, three German-manufactured stained glass windows commissioned by the United Daughters of the Confederacy memorialized Jefferson, his wife, Varina, and daughter, Winnie Davis.

The most striking feature of the Church of the Redeemer was its corner bell tower, a forty-five-foot-tall brick structure with arches sheltering bells. The original bell, supposedly taken from an old coastal plantation, was replaced with a memorial to World War II's soldiers in 1946.

In August 1969, Hurricane Camille destroyed all but the 1854 parish house and the bell tower. Church members dug through the rubble for shards of stained glass and shattered pews. They recovered Jefferson Davis's pew, recognizable by the silver nameplate. The parish house was reconsecrated to serve as the sanctuary once again, and the bell tower was left standing alone as a symbol of the coast's resilience.

Nature wasn't through with the bell tower. In the 1990s, lightning flashed down and struck the metal cross on top, setting the wooden roof on fire. The fire was extinguished and the cross replaced, this time with the addition of a lightning rod.

First Baptist Church of Greenwood

For most of the twentieth century, the skyline of Greenwood was dominated by two soaring landmarks: the multistaged tower of the Leflore County Courthouse and the finial-capped silver dome of First Baptist Church. The courthouse tower, with its four clock faces, remains, but the Baptist dome is long gone.

During Greenwood's formative years, the Methodists, Baptists, Presbyterians, and Masons shared space in the Union Church and Lodge, just south of the Yazoo River. Missionary Baptist Church moved into the old courthouse in July 1888, and occupied its own building in 1895. That twenty-five-hundred-dollar frame sanctuary was inadequate to hold the expanding congregation, growing with the wave of cotton prosperity in the first decade of the century. Greenwood had become the state's largest cotton market, and its population more than doubled between 1900 and 1907. In 1910, the renamed First Baptist Church dedicated a new sanctuary, on the northwest aspect of what would later be designated as the Four Corners Historic District.

The new building was an impressive brick structure with a tetrastyle portico, colossal fluted columns and pilasters, and a full entablature running around the perimeter of the entire building. Rectangular, arched, and square windows were filled with stained glass. The structure itself was imposing, but its crowning glory, literally, was the

First Baptist Church, Greenwood, ca. 1950. Photo courtesy of Sara Criss.

multitiered silver dome rising from the center of the roof. Four graduated sections soared high above the ground, capped with a huge finial.

A new sanctuary was completed in 1976, and the old one was neglected and gradually abandoned. The great dome began to shift under its own weight, and church members were increasingly reluctant to risk standing inside underneath its rotunda. The cost of shoring up the sagging landmark was prohibitive, and, despite its emotional significance, the entire building was razed in the late 1980s.

Chapter Four

Public Buildings

WHEN MISSISSIPPI TOOK ITS FIRST TENTATIVE STEPS toward statehood, it was a land of log cabins and dogtrot simplicity. Hundreds of miles from the centers of culture along the East Coast, Mississippians had to establish their own towns and push back the wilderness before they could embark on the architectural legacy which would come to symbolize the state's antebellum years.

In the early 1820s, the vast majority of Mississippi's population was clustered in the southwestern counties along the Mississippi River and in Gulf Coast villages. A few intrepid settlers had moved into the prairies bordering the Tombigbee River in northeast Mississippi. Following a succession of Indian treaties between 1820 and 1832, millions of acres of arable land opened up for development, and thousands of immigrants poured in from the Carolinas, Georgia, and Tennessee.

Counties were carved out of the acreage and county seats designated, traditionally in the geographic center of the county but often wherever a tiny settlement had managed to survive long enough to attract a store or a tavern. Once the county seat was determined, the first order of business was building a courthouse, often as not a rude log cabin where disputes could be settled and taxes paid. As soon as economic conditions permitted, these small buildings were usually replaced by more permanent, grander courthouses, often the most dominant structure for miles around.

In 1822, the shabby little settlement on the Pearl River at LeFleur's Bluff was chosen as the site for the new state's permanent capital city. It was far from being an instant success. For ten years, Jackson was just a mosquito plagued backwater, avoided by legislators unless they absolutely had to meet at the modest block statehouse on Capitol Street. The town had a couple of boardinghouses, a tavern, and a

State Insane Asylum
(See page 120.)

few homes, but no schools, churches, or significant businesses. When the legislature left each year, the village dried up. Serious consideration was given to moving the whole operation elsewhere.

The 1832 constitutional convention gave Jackson a temporary reprieve. It would retain its status as capital until 1850, but if no significant growth or development had occurred in that time, the legislature would be free to move elsewhere. Vicksburg, Clinton, and Natchez seemed more attractive options. With the treaties of Dancing Rabbit Creek and Pontotoc, towns were popping up all over the central and northern areas of the state, and soon they, too, would be competing for attention. Jacksonians realized that they had to do something fast to assure their continued claim as the capital city.

Governor Abram Scott led the move to erect permanent, monumental state buildings in Jackson. With his backing, the 1833 legislature passed "[a]n Act to provide for the erection of a State House and other public buildings in the town of Jackson, and for other purposes" and "a suitable house for the governor." Work was begun on the statehouse in 1834 and was finally completed in 1840. The Governor's Mansion followed, welcoming Tilghman Tucker as its first occupant in 1841. These two enduring symbols of state pride, designed by state architect William Nichols, were soon joined by the State Penitentiary and State Lunatic Asylum, admittedly less pleasant in purpose but no less notable architecturally than the mansion or the capitol. Jackson's future was secure, now carved in stone and embedded in bricks.

As Mississippi passed from frontier status to being one of the nation's most prosperous outposts, its developing social structure was reflected in its public buldings. Log courthouses disappeared, replaced by columned brick edifices worthy of the proud towns which claimed them. The statehouse at the foot of Capitol Street became a powerful symbol of antebellum pride and the gathering place for secessionists and political rallies. The penitentiary and asylum were enlarged and eventually rambled over dozens of acres.

An unfortunate consequence of the Civil War was that oftentimes the largest and most elaborate building in a town, whether it was the courthouse or the college or a church, was pressed into service as a hospital. Many were lost during the war, burned by one side or the other, accidentally or deliberately. Reconstruction saw a spate of rebuilding projects, and most of those edifices lasted until the twentieth century, when their Victorian exuberance was deemed outdated and many were gradually replaced.

The capitol was neglected and abandoned altogether at one point, nearly caving in on itself before it was rehabilitated for state offices. The State Penitentiary was demolished to make way for a more modern capitol. The sprawling State Insane Asylum, plagued from its earliest days by structural instability, was replaced with the University of Mississippi Medical Center; only a few graves and a host of legends remain to mark the asylum's history on North State Street.

State Penitentiary

William Nichols, the state architect responsible for the Old Capitol, the Governor's Mansion, the Lyceum at Ole Miss, and other antebellum masterpieces, was also the guiding force behind a more ominous Jackson landmark. While he was supervising the construction of the statehouse and the chief executive's house, his workers were toiling away on a Gothic fortress a few blocks north of Capitol Street. Nichols's State Penitentiary was a dark, brooding hulk, a drastic contrast to his soaring capitol and graceful mansion.

Mississippi was a rough place in its infancy. Small towns with barely enough populace to support a few businesses or build a log courthouse were plagued with lawbreakers. Since territorial days, Mississippi's governors had urged the legislature to fund a penitientiary. Gerard Brandon pled in 1827: "It may be the policy of the legislature at as early a period as our resources will justify, to establish a penitentiary . . . to reform the offender, and at the same time to protect society from a repetition of these offence[s]—these can be effectually accomplished only through the medium of a penitentiary."[1]

Governor Brandon's suggestions went unheeded by a legislature still unsure as to whether the capital's future even lay in Jackson. But with the rising walls of the capitol and the Governor's Mansion lending legitimacy to Jackson's supremacy, the bill authorizing the penitentiary was finally signed by Governor Charles Lynch in 1836. With so much building going on downtown, the work was slow, and it would be four years before the prison was ready for occupancy. When "the east prison contain[ed] 150 cells on three stories conformable to the Auburn system of prison discipline,"[2] the doors opened. Ireland native William McBride, given seven years for manslaughter,

Old State Penitentiary, ca. 1890. Photo courtesy of MDAH.

was prisoner number one. Before his sentence was finished, he had been joined by 220 other inmates, with an average of 85 incarcerated at any one time. The oldest was 106 years old when he was sentenced.

The prison itself was ominous enough to discourage most criminals. Towers and battlements loomed over the four-story cell block, and the grounds were filled with the din of cotton- and wool-milling machinery, blacksmith shops, carpentry and wheelwright sheds, and a brickyard. Some historians attribute antebellum Jackson's lack of industrial development to the "free labor" competition from the penitentiary.

When the Civil War started, the prison was converted to a munitions plant and repair center for cannons, rifles, and other weapons. Some of the prisoners were transferred to Alabama, while forty were pardoned and mustered into the Confederate Army. Sherman's troops set fire to the complex in May 1863, leaving it charred rubble.

The rebuilding of the penitentiary was a subject of debate following the war's end; Mississippi was in ruins and other needs took precedence. Given the lack of jail facilities, the constitutional convention went so far as to suggest automatic hanging for grand larceny, robbery, rape, arson, and burglary. The legislature decided instead to appropriate thirty thousand dollars for rebuilding. By 1866, there were 131 inmates in the new jail, most assigned to brickmaking duty.

The convict leasing system which developed during Reconstruction was a source of extreme abuse. It was justified by the crowding in the penitentiary; if prisoners were leased to Delta planters and railroad builders, they weren't taking up cell space. But the horrors of the undersupervised system became so blatant that by 1872 Governor Powers was calling for the construction of a prison farm. Land was actually purchased just north of Jackson on a five-hundred-acre site, but the financial panic of 1873 put a stop to those plans. It would be another twenty-five years before serious moves were discussed.

The need for more space wasn't the only threat to the viability of the State Penitentiary. The old state capitol was crumbling. Legislators intent on building a new statehouse eyed the prime penitentiary property enviously. General Stephen D. Lee called for a committee to investigate "the advisability of the state retaining the present penitentiary property as a location for the new capitol."[3] The ominous penitentiary squatted on one of the most desirable blocks of land in Jackson, and many Jacksonians considered its presence, just two blocks behind the Govenor's Mansion, an embarrassment. By 1896, the capitol was visibly deterioriating, with the third-floor library floor sagging beneath tons of discarded papers and books. Visitors and legislators avoided the room beneath it for fear of the ceiling crashing around their heads. Several wagonloads of paper were shipped to the penitentiary for storage, with debate raging on as to whether to tear down the Old Capitol and rebuild on Capitol Green or move a few blocks to the penitentiary site.

The decision was finally made in 1900, when the legislature appropriated one million dollars for a new capitol. Four thousand acres of Sunflower County land was purchased for the new penitentiary. By 1901, four stockades and several camps were complete at Parchman and the transfer of prisoners began. The walls of the old prison were pulled down, and the New Capitol, modeled on the national Capitol in Washington, D.C., went up. Legend holds that some of the odd, Indian-mound-like slopes on the grounds are sections of the vanished penitentiary, too deeply imbedded in the dirt ever to be removed.

State Insane Asylum

The University of Mississippi Medical Center is a labyrinthine complex of buildings occupying a sloping hill in Jackson. Deep within the basement of its original 1955 core are doorways which won't close and walls that meet at odd angles. Legend has it that this part of the med center was built atop the old tunnels which once connected the wings of the State Insane Asylum. Legend or not, the asylum's shadow hovers over the campus, most dramatically in the wooded burial ground between the medical library and St. Dominic Hospital.

The 1848 legislature authorized "that a lunatic asylum shall be established in this State, to be located in or near the city of Jackson."[4] The initial appropriation was for ten thousand dollars, which was partially used to purchase five acres at the north city limits. That site was deemed unsuitable, and 140 acres were bought two miles north of town for seventeen hundred dollars. Under the direction of architect William Gibbons, ground was broken and work began, the bricks being supplied by State Penitentiary inmates.

Gibbons designed a building larger and grander than that envisioned by the legislature, modeling it on the New Jersey asylum, with a central block and two long wings. Excavation, bricking, carpentry, and ironwork dragged on at a snail's pace for two years, as Gibbons ran through money and returned again and again to the legislature for more funds. By 1850, the first-floor walls were partially completed, and Gibbons was demanding another fifty-thousand-dollar appropriation. The legislature had run out of patience. A new board of commissioners was appointed; they fired Gibbons, hiring Joseph Willis as his replacement.

Willis inherited a mess. He left a record of his dismay with the quality of Gibbons's work:

> About the first of July, 1850, I was informed that the foundations had been laid, and the walls of the cellar . . . raised to the height of eight feet . . . As the work had been suspended for several months, the cellar was filled with water to the depth of from two to three feet.

State Insane Asylum, ca. 1900. Photo courtesy of MDAH.

After having the cellar drained, I discovered that the foundations under the walls were very soft, and as they began to dry, that the walls cracked in many places, from top to bottom . . . Under these circumstances, I was unwilling to put up the building, on the walls that had been erected, being satisfied that the foundations would not support the superincumbent weight of so massive a building; and that it would not be long before serious injury to the building would be caused by uneven settlements in the foundations . . .

Willis was also plagued by Yazoo clay, and provided an early description of the shifting soil which would aggravate Jacksonians for generations: "After the walls were removed . . . I found that the walls had been built on a bed of marl, that extends to the depth of from twenty to thirty feet, and that when it is wet, expands and becomes soft and slippery, and that when dry, it contracts and becomes hard, and if exposed to the atmosphere, crumbles or slacks like lime; consequently, it is a very poor material for foundations of buildings."[5]

Willis's problems were just beginning. As the massive three-story center block rose on the unsteady soil, fires, water problems, and a yellow fever epidemic slowed the work. Finally, in 1855, the hospital was ready for its first patients, with Willis surpris-

State Insane Asylum, ca. 1880. Photo courtesy of MDAH.

ingly not among those admitted. The commissioners proudly reported to the governor on the finished structure:

> The main or centre building, together with both wings, have been completed and the entire outside stuccoed, so that the whole structure presents an attractive appearance, both in finish and style of architecture, and will stand an enduring monument of the wisdom and benevolence of our noble State. Back buildings, substantially built of brick, have been completed for engine room, kitchen, wash room and for generating gas, and all the necessary apparatus for generating gas and steam are in successful operation. . . . Some fifty acres of ground have been enclosed, with a plain but substantial board fence, and a sufficiency cleared for pleasure and promonade [*sic*] grounds for the patients.[6]

The asylum had been operating for only a year when fire swept through it in 1856. The legislature appropriated sixteen thousand dollars for repairs. Seven years later, the hospital sat on the fringes of the fight for occupation of Jackson. It was outside the circle of Confederate defenses, leaving it to Union occupation. The patients were removed, and Federal soldiers climbed into the towering center cupola to signal their forces. Confederate fire rained down on the asylum. In exasperation, the hospital superintendent requested that both sides honor the neutrality of the building, and this request was honored, leaving the asylum with minimal damage.

Following the war, serious structural problems tormented those responsible for the asylum. A destructive fire and tornado damage added to their worries. The patient population was increasing, and two new wings were added, raising the capacity to three hundred beds. The overcrowding was alleviated somewhat in 1882, when East Mississippi State Hospital opened in Meridian.

By the end of the century, almost twelve hundred patients were crowded into the main building, numerous wings, and accessory buildings of the State Insane Asylum. One hundred ten employees scurried about the complex, and a training school for psychiatric nurses was added. Dunbar Rowland described the impressive campus: "This institution is situated on rising ground two miles north of the capitol, the building crowning a slope of beautiful lawn several acres in extent. The main building consists of an imposing center, four stories in height with handsome facade of columns. On each side are wings three stories high, connected by smaller four story divisions, two on one side and three on the other. Behind the main building are the annexes for colored patients, two for male, and two for female patients. These buildings are of plain, architectural design, but very comfortable and substantial."[7]

An insurance map of the era shows a huge circular pond, burial grounds, coal sheds, bake shops, print shops, carriage houses, and a variety of other outbuildings scattered around the campus.

Structural problems and overcrowding worsened. Mental health professionals were lobbying for an updated facility of multiple "wards" in freestanding buildings. The State Insane Asylum had outlived its usefulness in less than a century. In 1926, funds were appropriated to build a new complex in Rankin County, named after Governor Henry L. Whitfield. The patients were moved in 1935, leaving the eighty-year-old North State Street complex empty. It was demolished in the 1950s to make way for the University of Mississippi Medical Center.

Natchez Charity Hospital

The origins of the Natchez Charity Hospital can be traced back to the earliest days of the river city, when, in 1805, an institution was founded for the care of sick and

Natchez Charity Hospital, ca. 1870. Photo courtesy of the Thomas and Joan Gandy Collection.

indigent boatmen marooned in Natchez. In 1837, Congress authorized the construction of seven hospital buildings along the Mississippi and Ohio rivers. Natchez, being one of the busiest ports in the nation, was a logical locale for one of the seven.The building was designed by Robert Mills, architect of the Washington Monument, U.S. Treasury Building, and the Washington, D.C., post office. Construction began in 1849 and was not completed until 1852. Soon after, the hospital was designated a state institution.

During the Civil War, numerous large buildings around the state were commandeered for hospital service and then burned. Natchez Hospital was spared this fate by the lack of military action in the area. After the surrender of Vicksburg, Union officers used it as an administrative headquarters.

In the years of Reconstruction, the hospital found new purpose. The Saints' Baptist Missionary Association chartered Natchez Seminary in 1869, resolving to work "for the maintenance of liberty and elevation of our race."[8] They purchased the old hospital from the city of Natchez and converted it to a multipurpose classroom, dormitory, and faculty house. The school rapidly outgrew the building and moved to

Jackson in 1883. It would grow into Jackson College and, eventually, Jackson State University.

Natchez took over control of the hospital once again. In 1884, it was reopened as a charity hospital and continued in that role for almost one hundred years. An innovative three-year nursing education program was initiated in 1903, leading to the establishment of the Mississippi Nurses' Association. The state of Mississippi took control in 1920 and operated the Natchez Charity Hospital until it was closed because of safety violations in the early 1980s. Ironically, one of the primary hazards was the grand curving stair, rising five floors to the eight-sided cupola. Tube-style fire escapes were deemed inadequate.

The building was empty and awaiting restoration when it burned on August 4, 1984.

McCutchen House (Street Clinic)

William McCutchen bought the elaborate two-story Federal-style house at the corner of Vicksburg's Crawford and Monroe streets in 1860. Just three years later, he would be fleeing to cave shelters with his family of seven. During the Siege of Vicksburg, the home was headquarters for the Confederate general Carter L. Stephenson. The McCutchens moved back in soon after the surrender of Confederate forces on July 4, 1863.

McCutchen was a prosperous grocer and dealer in caskets. After his death in 1875, his wife stayed on in the home with her three unmarried daughters. Following her death in 1885, all three of the daughters married, and the house was sold to Dr. D. P. Street in 1903. Street added two floors and extended the south and east walls to house one of Mississippi's first privately owned hospitals and the South's first nursing school.

In 1942, the Sisters of Mercy took over the facility and renamed it Mercy Hospital. It was one of two state hospitals designated to admit polio victims and was the scene of chaos in December 1953, when a devastating tornado raked downtown Vicksburg, ripping through a crowded movie theater and injuring dozens of children. In 1957, the Sisters moved to the larger and more modern facility that would grow into Mercy Regional Medical Center, leaving the old McCutchen home to serve as Sydney House, a convalescent home.

McCutchen House (Street Clinic) (structure on right rear), ca. 1940. Photo courtesy of Old Courthouse Museum, Vicksburg.

McCutchen House (Street Clinic), ca. 1870. Photo courtesy of Dannie Weatherby.

McCutchen House (Street Clinic), ca. 1900. Photo courtesy of Dannie Weatherby.

Sydney House closed in 1993. Vagrants took over the abandoned building, which was destroyed by fire in a July 1995 blaze. Lost deep within the walls of the former hospital was the original McCutchen House.

Calhoun County Courthouse

Calhoun County was carved from portions of Chickasaw, Lafayette, and Yalobusha counties in March 1852. Mr. Gaston, a land speculator, donated 160 acres near the center of the new county for its seat of government, and the small community of Pittsboro gradually evolved with hotels and businesses to support the inevitable onslaught of lawyers and landowners.

By December of 1852, supervisors were looking at bids for the building of a courthouse. Financial setbacks and political squabbling delayed the completion of the building until 1855. When finally completed, the Calhoun County Courthouse was a classic, two-story temple-form brick structure with inset monumental columns. Total cost of its construction was approximately eight thousand dollars.

The courthouse was only six years old when Mississippi left the Union. Like other seats of government, it became the center of local commotion over the crisis:

Calhoun County Courthouse, ca. 1910. Photo courtesy of Calhoun County Historical and Genealogical Society.

A convention was called in Calhoun County to send delegates to the State Convention. The county convention met in the courthouse at Pittsboro and the old building reverberated with excitement, tumult and danger. At one stage of the proceedings a dispute arose and one wing of those who were opposed to secession bolted the convention and marched to the old Methodist church where they proceeded with their business. Colonel Sumner and Colonel M. D. L. Stephens were finally selected as the county delegates and were sent to the State Convention instructed to vote against secession. This they did on every ballot until it was clearly evident that they had lost. On the last ballot they changed their votes to "Yea" in order to make the action unanimous.[9]

Three years later, many were probably regretting that action. War had crept as close as Yalobusha County. The town's leaders were concerned about the safety of the county's records, and recruited sixteen-year-old Jim Harrelson to spirit them away to a safer place. Harrelson recounted his adventure many years later:

> In the month of March, 1864, a column of Yankee soldiers out on a plundering expedition had left the main body of Federal troops near Holly Springs and headed south. It was reported that they were making their way to our county. The little town of Pittsboro looked like a forsaken thing in an endless stretch of desert. The March wind whistled sharply around the corners of the forsaken buildings, which had been left in many instances to the mercy of goats and now & then a creaking shutter on the courthouse banged to with a snap. In the afternoon of this particular day, I was standing on the street corner looking away toward Coffeeville from whence the distant dull boom of cannons was waited on the air, for the report was true and a battle was being fought a little North of Coffeeville. I was approached by Judge J. S. Ryan, who wanted to know if I could drive an ox wagon on a particular errand . . . "I want you to load all the records of our county into the wagon and take them to a point in the Yallobusha [*sic*] bottom which 'old Sam' will show you." I told him I would take them . . . I drove up to the fence that then surrounded the Court House at the East side, and with the help of several men, piled everything that looked like county records, deed books, etc., into the great bed of the wagon. When I left the streets, it was late in the afternoon and . . . I felt very lonely, for there was no one with me.[10]

Young Harrelson completed his hazardous journey and, with the help of an elderly slave, hid the Calhoun County records beneath the floorboards of an old house. He related the outcome of his efforts: "The war ended. . . . [A]fter a year or so of hopeless misery and despair under the carpet bag rule, the county of Calhoun began to stand on a slight footing, and after another year or so of steady gaining, the books, records, deeds, etc. that I had hidden were brought back, but they were so hopelessly mixed up that the County employed Judge Duberry to straighten them up, which took him something like a year."[11]

The courthouse weathered war and Reconstruction and several decades following, but was in sad shape by 1908. Controversy raged over whether to repair it or build a new one. In its April 1908 issue, the *Calhoun City Clipper,* perhaps with an eye toward snagging the seat of government for its hometown, flatly declared the old structure "terribly inadequate and too dilapidated to repair."

The problem resolved itself when the 1855 courthouse burned in December 1922. The January 4, 1923, *Monitor-Herald* described the scene:

> Passersby noticed a light in the upper story of the Courthouse about ten o'clock or later on the night of the fire, but thinking it was members of the Sheriff's office working late, did not

> attach any importance to this fact. The Sheriff used the courtroom on the upper floor of the courthouse for office room and frequently he and deputies work late at night with the tax books this time of the year. It developed that none of the county officials returned to the building after supper time, and that all the fires in the stoves and in the fire-places were almost entirely out at the time they departed for their homes. From the manner in which the fires seem to have started and the fact that no fires were left in the building, as well as the manner in which the fire burned, including sounds of explosions in the lower offices, Sheriff Young as well as practically all the first arrivals on the scene are of the opinion that the fire was incendiary . . . Chancery Clerk C. D. Ellard made a desperate effort to save the land records of the county. He entered his office by breaking a window and had started handing out books through the stifling and blinding smoke when an explosion in the office shattered the windows and caused sheets of flame to burst from them . . . He made his escape through the flames . . . barely escaping with his life.[12]

Ellard later noted that "most speculation is that some fellows with liquor charges filed against them in the circuit clerk's office set the fire to destroy the indictments."[13]

The county offices were moved into an old newspaper and mercantile building, which was renovated by the WPA in 1939.

Marshall County Courthouse

Marshall County was one of the entities drawn from the six million acres acquired in the 1832 Treaty of Pontotoc. In May 1836, Holly Springs was chosen as its county seat, and within two years the town had blossomed into the third-largest town in Mississippi, lagging behind only Natchez and Vicksburg.

The first "courthouse" in Holly Springs was no more than a small log cabin. This wouldn't suffice for long, with settlers and businessmen and especially lawyers pouring into the region. A more substantial building was soon necessary. Plans were drawn for a two-story brick building, topped with an octagonal cupola and Doric pilasters lining the north and south facades. Somewhere along the way, the building doubled in size and wound up as a clapboard structure, still claiming the cupola but now flanked with two-story porches.

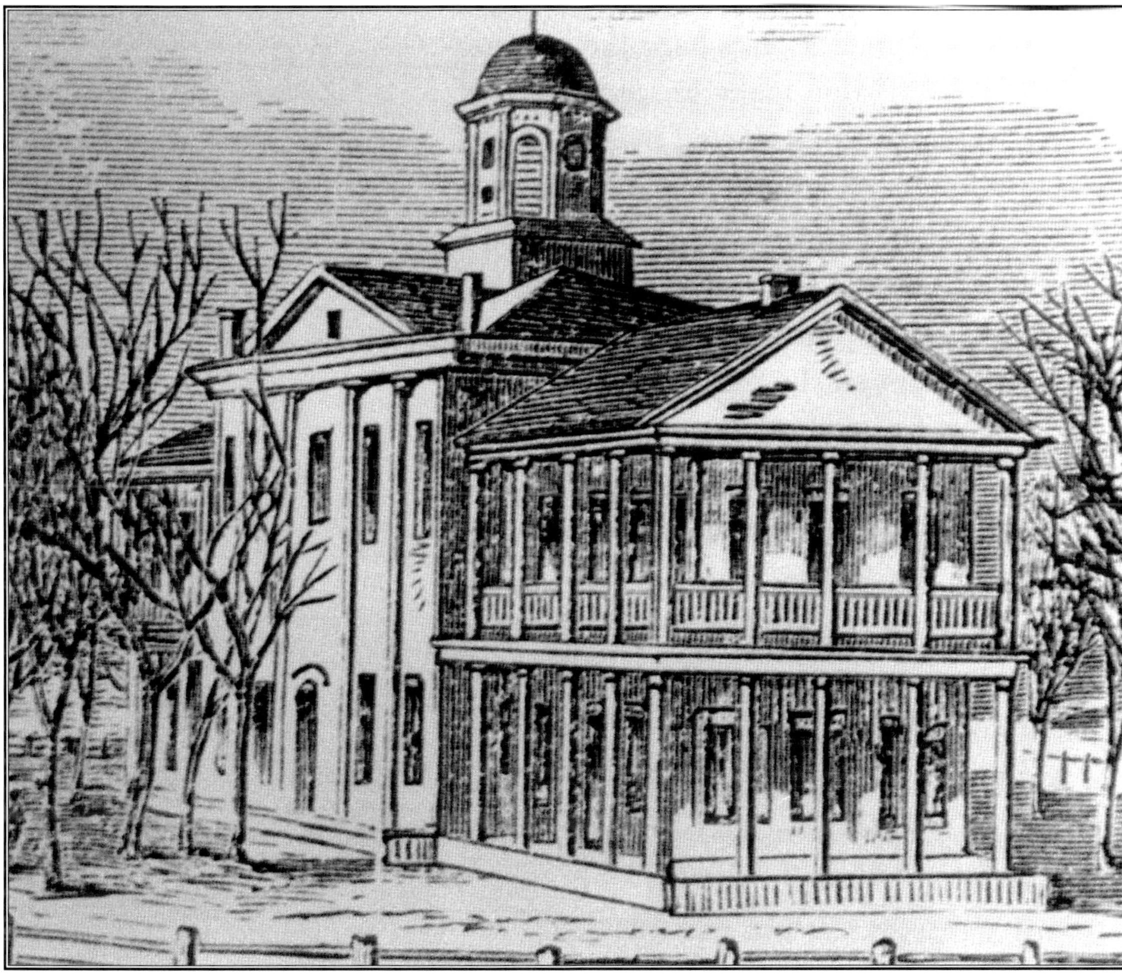

Marshall County Courthouse. Drawing from Harper's Weekly, ca. 1863. Photo courtesy of Chesley Thorne Smith.

When it was finished in 1838, at a cost of twenty-five thousand dollars, the Marshall County Courthouse was already the center of a booming square. Two hotels and eighteen stores lined the streets of Holly Springs. Forty lawyers vied for courtroom time. Visits by such luminaries as Sam Houston attracted huge crowds to lounge and picnic on the courthouse lawn.

Holly Springs was a flashpoint for the Civil War in Mississippi. General U. S. Grant marched through in the fall of 1862, claiming the town as his supply depot. He moved on toward Vicksburg, trusting a detail of troops to guard the munitions stored in businesses and churches around the square. Confederate General Earl Van Dorn considered this a taunt and an insult. His famous dawn raid on the sleeping town brought it back into Confederate hands, at least temporarily, but at a terrible cost. The Masonic Hall, just across the street from the courthouse, was blown, according to witnesses, several hundred feet into the air, setting most of the square aflame. Local Presbyterians, well aware that Grant had packed their new church with gunpowder and ammunition, cowered in their homes and waited for the explosion, which miraculously never came. The courthouse itself somehow survived the conflagration.

In 1864, a group of Union soldiers accidentally set the courthouse ablaze. The lawn stood empty for six years, until a Reconstruction government replaced the building with a new one. Modified over the years, it still serves Marshall County today.

DeSoto County Courthouse

Mississippi is renowned for its Greek Revival architecture, the very name conjuring images of columns and capitals and long verandas. But one of the most remarkable and unusual public buildings ever seen in Mississippi was a replica of a French castle, set down in the unlikely location of Hernando.

DeSoto was one of ten counties to develop from land sold to the United States government in the 1832 Treaty of Pontotoc. Hernando was designated the county seat, and citizens there followed the usual tradition of erecting a log cabin courthouse. It burned in the 1850s. Its replacement was a more substantial frame building, also lost to fire, this one set by Federal troops in 1863. Only one room remained, and all the offices of county government crowded into it for seven years.

Felix LaBauve was a native of France who had made his way to DeSoto County in 1838. A successful businessman and politician, his two passions were his adopted hometown and the University of Mississippi. LaBauve returned from a trip to France in 1870, carrying plans for a Norman castle. He persuaded the Reconstruction-era supervisors to fund the elaborate building, and E. Jones and Mathias Baldwin of Memphis were hired as architects.

Seven hundred fifty thousand bricks were molded and over forty thousand dollars budgeted for the new courthouse. Its towers and chimneys and arched entrances were

DeSoto County Courthouse, ca. 1920. Photo courtesy of Annie Ruth Brown.

unlike anything ever seen in north Mississippi. All went well until January 11, 1873, when the eighty-foot-tall tower collapsed. It was rebuilt and the "courthouse castle" completed. It would served DeSoto County for almost seventy years.

On the night of February 24, 1940, fire broke out in the tower. The alarms brought townspeople out in droves, and they scrambled into the burning building to throw county records out the windows as fire units from Hernando, Memphis, and Senatobia fought in vain to save the castle. It was unsalvageable and was subsequently razed to allow construction of the current courthouse.

Mississippi Institute for the Blind, ca. 1900. Photo courtesy of MDAH.

Mississippi Institute for the Blind

The hamlet of Sharon, in central Madison County, was a center for education in the mid-1800s. Several schools and colleges were established there, and the village rivaled Clinton in its reputation for academia. But Reverend James Champlain identified a need that was overlooked not only in Sharon but throughout Mississippi. Champlain was blind; it was his dream to have the state sponsor a school for the blind that would serve children with the same handicap.

Reverend Champlain lobbied the 1846 legislature to appropriate funds for the school. Finding that body unyielding, he opened his own school, the Chapin Institute, in a house on Jefferson Street in Jackson. The legislature finally came through in 1848, appropriating a twenty-five-hundred-dollar yearly stipend to support the school and officially designate it as the Mississippi Institute for the Blind.

By 1850, Reverend Champlain had five students in his school, and two years later the number was up to eleven. Recognizing the need for education for the blind, the legislature directed seven thousand dollars from the sale of public lands to enlarge the school. A music department was added, and the students were trained in broom making.

As was the case with most of the institutions in Jackson, the Civil War brought disruption. The institute for the blind was moved to Monticello for several years. In 1882, it settled into a grand new building on North State Street, the property bought with funds from Vicksburg native William C. Johnson's bequest. Consisting of three stories with multiple dormers and open porches, the school was topped with a two-stage tower. By 1889, enrollment was up to forty-three students, many remaining for the full ten-year curriculum. One of the teachers was Mrs. Phelps, the daughter of Civil War mayor Charles Manship, whose home backed up to the institute. She remained on the faculty for decades.

When the school at the institute for the deaf on West Capitol Street was condemned in 1939, administrators of both schools began to lay plans for a move to Eastover. The state owned property there which had once been part of the insane asylum's farm acreage. In 1946, ground was broken for a new campus to hold the institute for the deaf and the school for the blind. The old institute for the blind was outdated and located on a prime lot across from Baptist Hospital. It was demolished and the land used for hospital expansion.

Mississippi Institute for the Deaf

In 1829, the Mississippi legislature passed an act authorizing the spending of two hundred dollars for "sending children who were thought capable of receiving the benefits of an education at institutions established for that purpose."[14] This rather cryptic decree was intended to benefit young Thomas Kennon, a deaf mute from Marion County. Ideally, the state, lacking its own school for the deaf, would have sent any child with that handicap to a school that could accommodate him. The only documented deaf child to ever benefit from the act was Kennon, whose tuition at the Kentucky School for the Deaf was paid by the state.

Mississippi Institute for the Deaf (Yerger House), ca. 1890. Photo courtesy of MDAH.

Twenty-five years later, the Mississippi Institute for the Deaf and Dumb was finally chartered. Its trustees paid nine thousand dollars for the buildings of the Cleaver Female Institute on Capitol Street, just across from the Governor's Mansion. That property soon proved too small for the fifty students who were enrolled by 1857. A deal was struck with the Episcopal Diocese, owners of St. Andrew's College, and the campus of that school "about a mile west of the city limits on the road to Clinton"[15] became the new home of the institute for the deaf.

The students were sent home soon after the Civil War began. Their buildings became hospitals and then casualties of General Sherman's torch in 1863. For almost ten years, education for the deaf in Mississippi languished. The Reconstruction legislature purchased the mansion of George Shall Yerger on North State Street and converted it into a school for fifty students, opening it in 1871. Not long afterwards, eleven-year-old William Tompkins enrolled. He was a black child from Noxubee

Mississippi Institute for the Deaf, ca. 1905. Photo courtesy of MDAH.

County, handicapped by deafness, and he may have been the first African-American student ever to attend a white school in Mississippi. A school exclusively for deaf blacks was opened on the old St. Andrew's College site in 1882.

In 1902, the Yerger mansion burned, along with all of its outbuildings. None of the 165 students were hurt, but once again they were without a school. West Coast architect Olaf Hanson, who was also deaf, was chosen to design a new building for the institute. His creation, in the 1400 block of West Capitol, came to be a Jackson landmark. It was an enormous five-story brick edifice with fanciful twin towers and a neoclassic entrance. Numerous dormers pierced the mansard roof, and porches were added to the side elevations.

Enrollment at the school grew to the maximum of 175 students, all living in the sprawling complex with their teachers and administrators. A 1916 tornado took down one wing of the building, necessitating the spending of one hundred thousand dollars for repairs. More insidious damage had been occurring from the time of the school's opening, as the Yazoo clay beneath the foundation shifted and rolled. By 1939, the building had been officially condemned. With no place to send the students, the administration yearly filed away the grand jury's report that decreed the institute a fire

Wilkinson House (Fairgrounds Activity Building), ca. 1920. Photo courtesy of MDAH.

hazard and deathtrap. Walls pulled away from floors, the towers leaned, and the whole structure became increasingly precarious.

The 1946 legislature finally appropriated funds for a new campus. It was not completed until 1951, at which point the student body gratefully abandoned the teetering 1904 building. At salvage, 750,000 board feet of longleaf yellow pine lumber, 2 1/2 million bricks, 42 tons of steam radiators, and 140 tons of brass were auctioned. The grand old building took months to demolish, leaving its site vacant on West Capitol Street.

Wilkinson House (Fairgrounds Activity Building)

When Peter Van Dorn laid out the capital city of Jackson in 1822, he placed the statehouse on a broad green esplanade above the Pearl River. Capitol Street would run due west from the government building and house commercial and professional development. State Street would run north to south in front of the capitol and serve as the preferred residential thoroughfare.

Van Dorn's plan took years to see fruition, and it didn't always pan out as envisioned, but North State Street did become the showplace for Jackson's early wealth. No lot on that street has seen more history or significant structures than the northeast corner of Amite and North State. The Eagle Hotel was Jackson's first "real" hostelry, hosting Andrew Jackson in the 1840s and briefly housing the city's first school. Its successor, the Bowman House, was a revolving door for Confederate and Union generals in the dark days of spring 1863.

The Bowman House burned accidentally after Federal troops had left Jackson. Its ruins littered the lot for thirteen years as the owners squabbled in court. After they finally demolished the walls, the lot sat empty until 1903. Local businessman Dan Wilkinson hired New Capitol architect Theodore Link to design his new home on the prime site. Link built an imposing two-story frame house with balustraded porches. On the south facade, a three-storied tower with arched openings looked out over the Old Capitol.

Standard Oil bought the lot in the 1920s and built their local headquarters there. The Wilkinson House was moved down the hill to the fairgrounds, where it served for decades as the "women's building" or "activity building." It was demolished in midcentury.

Tippah County Courthouse

Many of William Faulkner's most memorable characters were based on family and acquaintances in northeast Mississippi. Faulkner's paternal great-grandfather, W. C. Falkner, led a rowdy life in Ripley that rivaled anything his descendant could invent.

Tippah County Courthouse, ca. 1900. Photo courtesy of Ripley Public Library.

The tombstone over a grave there claims its occupant was "Killed at Ripley, Miss. By Wm. C. Falkner, May 8, 1849." [16] Falkner served briefly as a Confederate officer, switched to the more profitable pursuit of blockade-running, authored a romantic novel, and traveled through Europe following the war. He joined with Richard J. Thurmond to build the Ripley Railroad Company, but the partnership soon dissolved in bitter feuding. In November 1889, Thurmond gunned Falkner down on the square, within sight of the Tippah County Courthouse.

Mr. Falkner's great-grandson would one day capture the essence of the court squares and their commanding centerpieces in Oxford and Ripley and countless other little towns across the South: "A Square, the courthouse in its grove the center; quadrangular around it, the stores, two-story, the offices of the lawyers and doctors and dentists, the lodgerooms and auditoriums, above them, school and church and tavern and bank and jail each in its ordered place; the four broad diverging avenues straight as plumb-lines in the four directions, becoming the network of roads and by-roads until the whole county would be covered by it."[17]

Ripley's square was home first to a crude log building, replaced in 1838 with a brick structure. That building was burned by Federal troops in 1864, along with a number of homes, including W. C. Falkner's. The new Tippah County Courthouse, completed under a Reconstruction regime, was a two-story brick block with balancing wings and a full-height Greek Revival portico.

Richard Thurmond's murder trial in the Tippah County Courthouse was probably the building's most dramatic moment. He was acquitted in February 1891. The courthouse stood for another thirty-seven years before it was replaced with a more modern building, which incorporated some of the architectural elements of the 1870 courthouse.

NEWMAN

Chapter Five

Industrial Sites

In a 1909 review of Mississippi's industrial history, University of Mississippi chemistry professor A. M. Muckenfuss presented a terse summary of the state's manufacturing legacy:

> The State of Mississippi never has been, and perhaps never will be, a manufacturing State in the sense that we use this expression towards States like Massachusetts, New York or Ohio. Its greatest wealth, probably, must always lie in its rich soils and the varied products of its lands. But a strictly agricultural State is not an ideal commonwealth; too many people have the same point of view. There is not enough friction of minds with different interests and varying aspirations to develop to the highest extent a great civilization. It is therefore devoutly to be hoped that the industrial life of Mississippi will continue to grow until a balance of power is maintained between the agricultural, mercantile and industrial classes. Then, indeed, will the great Constitution under which the State is now being governed reach its largest fruition.[1]

Mississippi was approaching the end of its first century of statehood when Professor Muckenfuss published his opinions in the Mississippi Historical Society journal. Oddly enough, in 1909, the state was in the midst of an era when it was a national leader in one particular field, the logging and milling of yellow pine lumber. But the professor's overall view was correct. From its inception, Mississippi was, and would remain for many years, an agricultural land.

Before the Civil War, the Industrial Revolution all but bypassed Mississippi. A huge majority of her people worked the land or were engaged in business in one of the numerous small towns or few cities scattered about the state. Available capital was

J. J. Newman Lumber Company
(See page 149.)

poured into land and slaves rather than factories. With cotton flowing out of Mississippi's fields, a few attempts were made to capitalize on its ready availability. John Robinson, a Scottish textile expert, came to Natchez in 1842 with plans to open a cotton mill. He managed to get the operation going and actually produced some coarse fabrics, primarily for slave clothes and bagging, before selling out to a Boston firm in 1844. The northern industrialists brought in their own workmen to install more modern steam engines. Using a mixed labor force of slaves and white mill workers from New England, they turned out cotton rope, bagging, and some clothing for a brief time. By 1847, the mill was closed for good.

James Wesson was more successful. A Georgia native with extensive experience in the fiber industry, he brought thirty families with him to start a cotton mill in Choctaw County. The workers built their own machinery; looms and steam engines were ordered from the North and production began in the fall of 1848. Wesson was an excellent manager, and the mill was consistently profitable throughout its sixteen-year existence. In 1861, he was overseeing a thousand spindles, twenty looms, and an accompanying grist mill and flour mill, known collectively as Missssissippi Manufacturing Company.

Wesson's chief competition came from the government of his adopted state. The State Penitentiary in Jackson had begun producing cotton yarns as early as 1840, using manual machinery to weave coarse prison clothing. In 1850, the legislature appropriated fourteen thousand dollars to update the equipment and gave the superintendent permission to sell surplus fabric at public auction. Until the Civil War, the operation was economically successful, generating enough surplus capital to help fund the prison. Fire destroyed the plant in 1857; not wanting to lose a profitable industry with a captive workforce, the legislature funded a new two-story brick building with twenty-three hundred spindles and seventy-six looms.

In Wilkinson County, Judge Edward McGehee formed Wilkinson County Manufacturing Company in 1851. The noted Weldon Brothers, architects of many of Mississippi's most notable antebellum buildings, designed the four-story cotton-processing plant and two-story wool-processing facility. Nearby were warehouses, offices, apartment houses for workers, and a boardinghouse. At the peak of its production, McGehee was running four thousand spindles and eighty looms, using local white labor and New Englanders.

When Mississippi seceded from the Union, the cotton mills shifted to war production. Judge McGehee produced uniforms and woolens for the Confederate troops; the

State Penitentiary facilities were converted to munition manufacture and repair. Federal troops swept into Mississippi in 1863, systematically destroying the penitentiary buildings, Green's Mill on the Pearl River, and Wilkinson County Manufacturing Company. Judge McGehee lost not only his factory but also his mansion, Bowling Green, torched by marauding Kansas troops. James Wesson's operation in Choctaw County was more isolated, but it, too, was discovered by Union troops and burned in 1864.

It would be thirty years before Mississippi saw another industrial trend. A network of railroads slowly advanced across the state in the 1880s and 1890s, and a few sawmills grew up alongside the tracks. In the 1890s, a rapidly expanding nation was consuming lumber at a remarkable rate, and a few visionary men saw the potential in south Mississippi's vast acres of virgin pine timber. Hattiesburg and Laurel grew up around huge outfits like J. J. Newman, Tatum, and L. N. Dantzler lumber companies. Smaller towns and villages popped up along the "dummy lines," offshoot railroads built specifically to haul the pine logs to the main tracks. Between 1880 and 1900, manufacturing concerns in the state grew from a mere 1,479 to almost 5,000, employing twenty-one thousand people, many of them in the logging and milling business. By 1905, the virgin forests in the Piney Woods region were disappearing at a phenomenal clip, and two-thirds of the state's manufacturing jobs involved wood in some form or another. Gulfport led the nation in shipments of yellow pine, and Mississippi ranked third in lumber production.

Such depletion of a natural resource, no matter how financially rewarding, could not continue. The U.S. Department of Agriculture saw the inevitable outcome in 1909: "The situation would be critical even if it meant the exhaustion of a great natural resource through close utilization and good methods of cutting. But inasmuch as cutting has been unusually severe and wasteful, and since fire almost invariably follows lumbering, more than half of the long leaf pine land of the State has been converted into a blackened and barren waste. This means that over the larger part of the area there is little or no reproduction of the timber which, when once gone, will not be replaced by a new growth, which should be now coming on, and that immigration has not been fast enough to put the cleared lands under cultivation."[2]

Mississippi's giant mills had killed the golden goose. The forests were stripped almost bare, and there was no other source of timber to feed their milling machinery. One by one, the mills slowed, cut back, and then closed. The tiny towns that had depended solely on logging dried up and vanished. Cities like Laurel and Hattiesburg, born of the lumber boom, had to find new sources of income for their people. In the

1930s, Governor Hugh White would initiate his Balance Agriculture with Industry program with some degree of success, but Mississippi's most intensely industrialized era was over.

Jones-McElwain Iron Foundry

Antebellum Mississippi was an overwhelmingly agricultural society, its prosperity measured in acreage and bales rather than tonnage or ships or finished products. But one notable exception, the Jones-McElwain Iron Foundry, brought forth cast-iron masterworks which still grace some of the finest mansions in Mississippi. It may have been fully operational for only a few years, but its blacksmiths turned out balcony grilles and fences and column capitals that still symbolize the Old South.

As early as 1843, there was an ironworking enterprise in Holly Springs. The 1850 census lists twelve blacksmiths and twenty-four men who were employed in some fashion with the industry. The census ten years later lists Jones-McElwain as an active foundry with $12,000 in capital investments and a hundred employees earning a total of $4,550 per month. In that last year of peace, Jones-McElwain produced 1,350 tons of iron castings, valued at $120,000, and 8 tons of brass work, valued at $8,000. Included in its inventory were rails for the Mississippi Central Railroad, grillwork for the Charles Bonner home, and decorative elements for West Point's Waverley and Aberdeen's French House. The raw iron was dug from Marshall County surface deposits; it was heated and bent over fires stoked from local hardwood charcoal. Corinthian and Ionic capitals and heavy iron window moldings were hauled overland to Wyatt Crossing, loaded onto Tallahatchie River steamboats, and sent on their way to New Orleans and Memphis. Plows were fashioned for local use.

The same week that Confederate gunners fired on Fort Sumter, Jones-McElwain completed the purchase of five plots of land just north of Holly Springs. The acreage surrounded a sprawling complex of factory buildings. The main block was two-storied, 300 feet by 40 feet with two 150-foot-long wings. The extra land may have been purchased in anticipation of expansion. A twenty-thousand-dollar contract with the Confederate government was signed, providing payment for the manufacture of small arms, including thirty thousand guns. Records are inconclusive as to whether any guns were ever actually made at Jones-McElwain; it may have engaged only in repair. In

Jones-McElwain Iron Foundry, ca. 1862. Photo courtesy of MDAH.

February 1862, the Confederate government formally purchased the foundry, and it recorded its last outgoing shipment in May of that year. In June, General Grant's troops occupied Holly Springs and used the foundry complex for munitions storage. Plans were made to convert it into a two-thousand-bed hospital, but those plans never saw fruition. On the morning of December 20, 1862, Confederate general Earl Van Dorn launched his lightning raid into Holly Springs. Jones-McElwain was one of the many buildings lost in the fires that followed. For years, the site yielded nails, hinges, and architectural hardware for scavengers and treasure seekers.

Mississippi Mills

On the map of Mississippi, there's a mysterious divot taken out of the northern edge of Lincoln County. Copiah County juts south, scoops up Wesson and Beauregard, and turns north again. This geographical anomaly can be traced back to the state's first successful industrialist, James Wesson, a man with enough clout to reroute political boundaries.

Wesson came to Mississippi in the 1840s with a scheme to use the young state's cotton production to manufacture cloth. He brought thirty cotton mill workers and their families from Georgia to rural Choctaw County, near the community of Drane's Mill. They built the necessary machinery and imported looms and steam engines from the Northeast. By 1849, Mississippi Manufacturing Company was processing three hundred pounds of raw cotton daily on five hundred spindles. Wesson plowed the profits back into the facility, opening a corn-grinding mill and flour mill and purchasing wool-carding machines.

For fifteen years, Wesson's cotton mill was the most productive and financially successful private enterprise of its kind in Mississippi. During the Civil War, it was far removed from the major battles fought in the state. Northern armies systematically destroyed mills in Jackson and Woodville, but didn't stumble across the Choctaw County plant until 1864. Then, like Green's Mill in Jackson and McGehee's Mill in Woodville, it was torched.

James Wesson regrouped and moved to south Mississippi. In 1866, he opened the first buildings of the rechartered Mississippi Manufacturing Company in the town which would come to bear his name, populating the tiny railroad stop with his workers and their families. Wesson was a vocal opponent of alcohol, and he wrangled the boundaries of the newly created Lincoln County so that his town would be left in dry Copiah. Houses were built, and stores soon followed. Captain William Oliver and John T. Hardy bought Wesson out in 1870, only to see the mill burn in 1873. They recruited the state's largest landowner, Edmund Richardson, as a partner and built a bigger and more modern plant, which would grow into what some sources claim was the largest cotton manufacturing mill south of Ohio.

Mississippi Mills, as the company came to be known, eventually expanded into three monumental brick buildings covering several acres, rivaling the great mills of New England in size and production. By the 1890s, all were in full operation, with more than a thousand employees. Generators lit the factory windows twenty-four hours a day, drawing curious sightseeers to marvel at the wonder of electric lights.

Dunbar Rowland described the mill and town when production was at its height:

Mississippi Mills, ca. 1910. Photo courtesy of MDAH.

> These mills have an excellent reputation and their product goes into nearly every State and Territory of the Union. The product is of great variety, and includes cassimeres, jeans, doeskins, tweeds, linseys, flannels, cottonades, flannellettes, gingham plaids, cheviots, checks, plaids, stripes, hickory, brown sheeting, shirting, drilling, eight ounce osnaburgs, ticking for feathers and mattresses, sewing thread, sewing twine for bags and awnings, wrapping twine, honey comb towels, awning, balmoral skirts, etc. The plant is equipped with an excellent system of water works, has an immense cotton warehouse, with a capacity of 1,000 bales of cotton, and storage for two million pounds of wool. In 1904 it manufactured 3,737 bales of cotton.[3]

Within two years of Rowland's tour, a series of missteps shut down Mississippi Mills. The machinery was creaking and outdated. Labor unrest was growing, and the management had shifted from Mississippi to out of state control. In 1906, the doors of the plant were closed. The towering buildings sat empty for fifteen years before being demolished. James Wesson's town, once the largest on the rail line between Jackson and New Orleans, dwindled in population and gradually lost almost all traces of its industrial birth. The only remnant of Mississippi Mills is a building housing the old packing and shipping rooms.

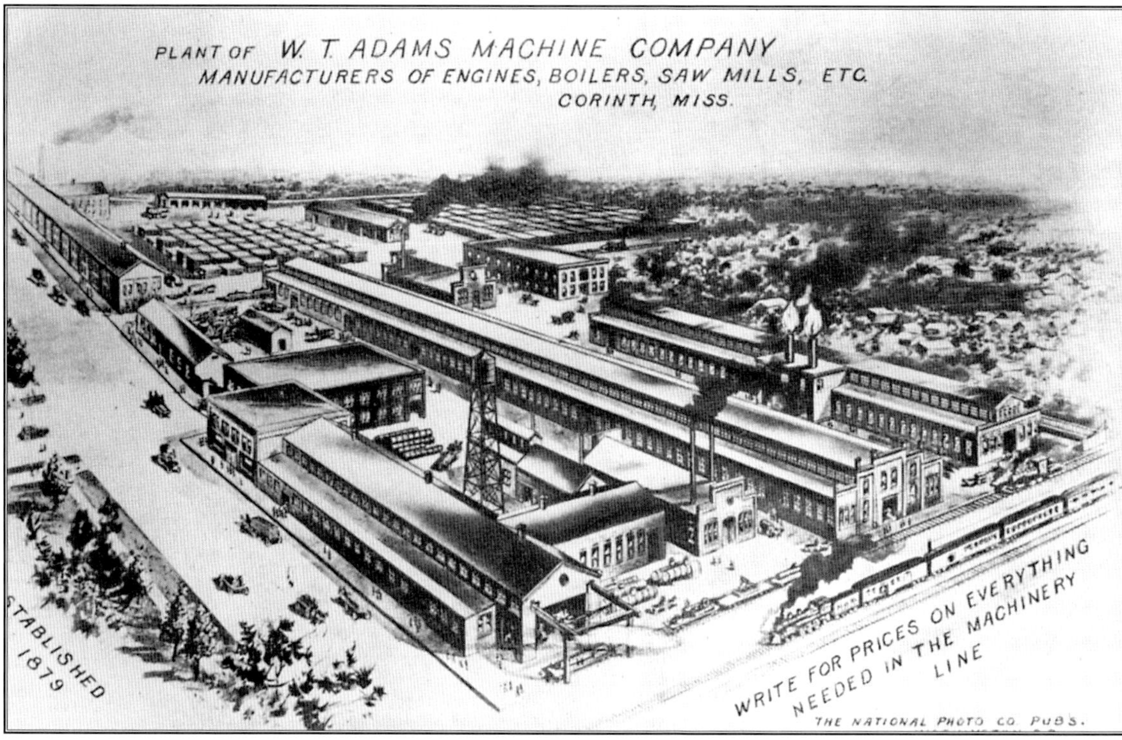

W. T. Adams Machine Company, ca. 1900. Photo courtesy of MDAH.

W. T. Adams Machine Company

Corinth's location at the junction of two major railroad lines gave birth to the town, but also brought the full fury of the Civil War into the town itself. By the 1870s, the area was recovering from war and Reconstruction, and those same rail lines led to a burst of industrial growth which was rare for Mississippi.

W. T. Adams Machine Company was founded in 1879 to produce boilers, engines, and sawmill equipment. Within a few years, its multitude of buildings had spread to cover acres of land along the Mobile and Ohio tracks. Five hundred employees labored in the long brick sheds. To benefit not only his workers but also the citizens of Corinth, Adams opened a public library in one of the plant's office buildings. Before it closed in 1912, it housed over a thousand volumes.

Most of the Adams Machine Company complex burned in 1917 and was not rebuilt.

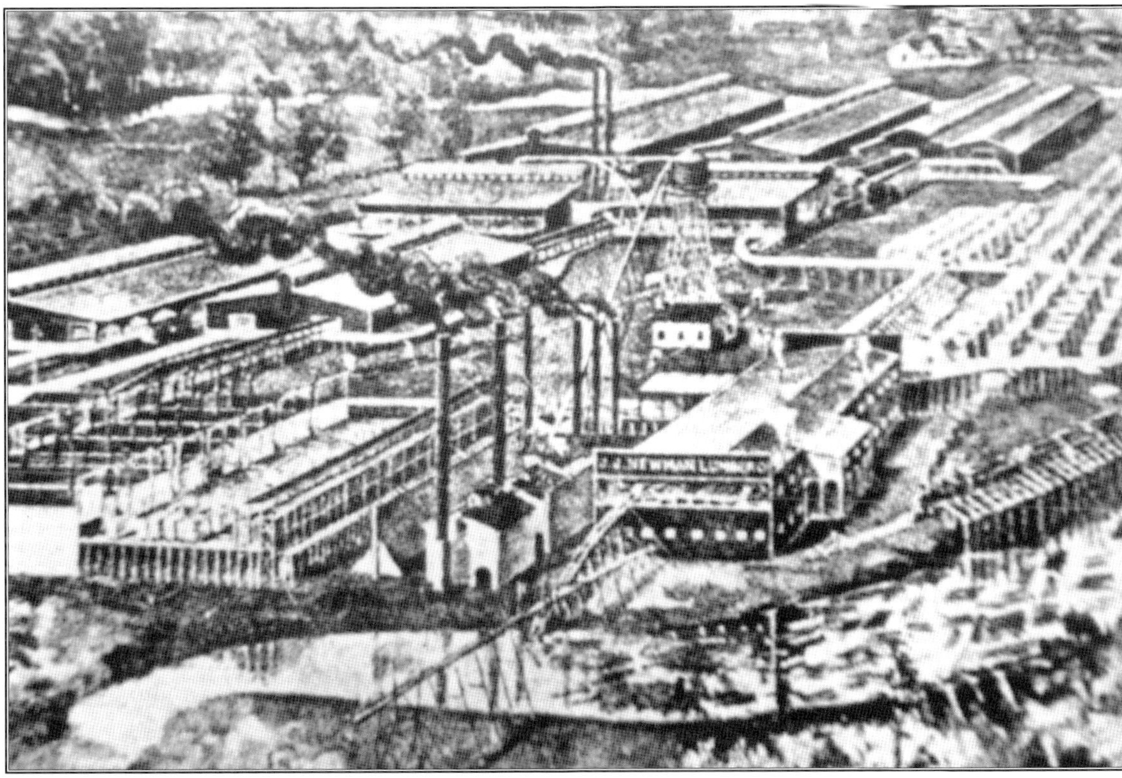

J. J. Newman Lumber Company, ca. 1920. Photo courtesy of MDAH.

J. J. Newman Lumber Company

The little town of Hattiesburg burned to the ground in 1893. The same fate had befallen its Wiscasset Lumber Mill earlier that same year. Hattiesburg rebuilt, ironically enough with a city ordinance decreeing that all commercial buildings must be fireproof. Within years, this town that discouraged wooden structures would be the world's center of yellow pine lumbering, cutting and milling and shipping more wood around the world than any other city.

The J. J. Newman Lumber Company was built on the banks of the Leaf River where the New Orleans and Northeastern Railroad crossed the water. Beneath it were the ashes of the old Wiscasset Lumber Mill. Newman rode the burgeoning interest in Mississippi's Piney Woods to financial success, and it caught the eye of Pennsylvania entrepreneur Fenwick Peck. Peck bought into the Mississippi operation and expanded it to include not only a maze of mill buildings, but also dozens of houses, offices, and support sheds for blacksmithing, carpentry, and machinery. The city-within-a-city produced its own electricity and owned an independent water system and fire department.

At the turn of the century, the J. J. Newman saws ran nonstop, occupying twelve hundred employees who turned out over two hundred thousand board feet of lumber per day. The company owned four hundred thousand acres in south Mississippi and logged it relentlessly, feeding the virgin pine into its mills at the rate of seventy-five million board feet each year. By 1915, the results were apparent. The forests were all but depleted, and loggers had to venture further and further to supply the mills. In another twenty years, there were no pine forests left to clear. J. J. Newman ceased operations, leaving the huge complex empty. In 1971, the last remaining office building burned. Only a house-sized iron safe remains of the state's largest lumber mill.

Notes

Chapter 1: Schools and Colleges

1. W. C. C. Claiborne, as quoted in David Sansing, *Making Haste Slowly: The Troubled History of Higher Education in Mississippi* (Jackson: University Press of Mississippi, 1990), 4.

2. George Poindexter, as quoted in Dunbar Rowland, *The Official and Statistical Register of the State of Mississippi: 1912* (Nashville, TN: Brandon Printing Co., 1912), 284.

3. John Anthony Quitman, as quoted in Rowland, *Official and Statistical Register*, 285.

4. Joseph Holt Ingraham, as quoted in Rowland, *Official and Statistical Register*, 286.

5. Robert Milton Winter, *Shadow of a Mighty Rock* (Franklin, TN: Providence House, 1997), 51.

6. A. M. Clayton, as quoted in Winter, 51.

7. Alexander G. McNutt, as quoted in Rowland, *Official and Statistical Register*, 286.

8. Albert G. Brown, as quoted in William D. McCain, "Education in Mississippi in 1860," *Journal of Mississippi History* 22, no. 1 (1960): 153–66.

9. Edward Mayes, as quoted in Rowland, *Official and Statistical Register*, 287.

10. F. A. P. Barnard, as quoted in David Sansing, *The University of Mississippi: A Sesquicentennial History* (Jackson: University Press of Mississippi, 1999), 103.

11. Mrs. George Sulser, as quoted in Mrs. J. G. Johnson, "The University War Hospital," *Publications of the Mississippi Historical Society* 12 (1912): 94–106.

12. W. E. Small, as quoted in Ricky Harold Gray, "Corona Female College (1857–1864)," *Journal of Mississippi History* 42, no. 2 (1980): 129–34

13. Charles Clark, as quoted in Rowland, *Official and Statistical Register*, 247.

14. Robert Milton Winter, *Shadow of a Mighty Rock* (Franklin, TN: Providence House, 1997), 51.

15. Hodding Carter, *A Vanishing America: The Life and Times of the Small Town* (New York: Holt, Rinehart and Winston, 1964), 60.

16. F. A. P. Barnard, "Autobiographical Sketch of Dr. F. A. P. Barnard," *Publications of the Mississippi Historical Society* 12 (1912): 107–21.

17. F. A. P. Barnard, as quoted in Sansing, *University of Mississippi*, 103.

18. Rowland, *Official and Statistical Register,* 205.

19. Annie E. Jacobs, as quoted in Elmo Howell, *Mississippi Scenes* (Memphis: n.p., 1992), 172.

20. Susan Gaston, as quoted in *History of Old Tishomingo County*, n.p., n.d.

21. Maud Morrow, as quoted in Gray.

22. W. E. Small, as quoted in Gray.

23. Quotation from Hillman College Catalogue, 1889–90.

24. Hugh White, as quoted in Roy V. Scott and Charles D. Lowery, *Old Main: Images of a Legend* (Goshen, KY: Harmony House Publishers, 1995), 20.

25. Charles Ayer, as quoted in Lelia G. Rhodes, *Jackson State University: The First Hundred Years* (Jackson: University Press of Mississippi,1979), 28.

26. Marcia Gibbs, as quoted in James F. Gordon, Jr., *A History of Belhaven College* (Greenwood: Mississippi Printing Company, 1983), 2.

27. Kate Markham Power, as quoted in Gordon, 3–4.

28. Quotation from unnamed author, "Heights Academy Closed for Five Years, But 'Prof's' Widow Keeps Up With Boys," *Tupelo Daily Journal*, 5 August 1954.

Chapter 2: Hotels and Spas, Springs and Resorts

1. Unnamed source, as quoted in D. Clayton James, *Antebellum Natchez* (1968; reprint, Baton Rouge: Louisiana State University Press, 1993), 189.

2. Joseph Holt Ingraham, as quoted in Samuel B. Olden, Jr., "Hotels, Inns and Taverns in Mississippi, 1830–1860," *Journal of Mississippi History* 5, no. 4 (1943): 171–84.

3. Ibid.

4. J. T. Wharton, as quoted in Carroll Brinson, *Jackson: A Special Kind of Place* (Jackson, MS: Hederman Brothers, 1977), 67–68.

5. Preston Cooper, as quoted in Gordon Cotton, "Cooper's Well, Once-Famous Resort," *Vicksburg Evening Post*, 30 June 1974.

6. Advertisement in 1850 *Madisonian*, as quoted in local history by James B. Lacey, Jr.

7. Unknown member of Fourteenth Infantry, as quoted in Brinson, 68.

8. *Along the Gulf* (1895; reprint, Pass Christian Historical Society, 1991).

9. Ibid.

10. Quotation from advertising brochure for Great Southern Hotel, 1903.

11. Thomas Rodney, as quoted in *The Pennsylvania Magazine of History and Biography* 43 (1919): 290–310.

12. J. T. Wharton, as quoted in Brinson, 67–68.

13. Ibid.

14. Quotation from *Jackson Daily News*, 11 June 1863.

15. Unknown member of Fourteenth Infantry, as quoted in Brinson, 68.

16. William T. Sherman, as quoted in Brinson, 109.

17. Quotation from *Along the Gulf*.

18. Preston Cooper, as quoted in Hubert Spengler's history of Cooper's Well, excerpts printed in *Jackson Daily News*, 3 March 1949.

19. Ibid.

20. Ibid.

21. Ibid.

22. Ibid.

23. Ibid.
24. Ibid.
25. Unknown writer, "B," as quoted in *Hinds County Gazette*, 24 August 1859.
26. Advertising brochure for Cooper's Well.
27. Advertisement in 1850 *Madisonian,* as quoted in local history by James B. Lacey, Jr.
28. Elizabeth Hatheway, as quoted in Carol Lynn Mead, *The Land Between Two Rivers* (Canton, MS: Friends of the Madison County–Canton Public Library, 1987), 199.
29. Quotation from *Along the Gulf.*
30. Ibid.
31. Ibid.
32. Quotation from J. S. Rea in insurance register of Rea Insurance Agency, Wesson, Mississippi, 1882.
33. WPA file on Owens Wells, Mississippi Department of Archives and History.
34. *Mississippi: The WPA Guide to the Magnolia State* (1938; reprint, Jackson: University Press of Mississippi, 1988), 426–27.
35. Ibid., 395.
36. Ibid., 484–85.
37. James Lacey, Jr., "Blaze Destroys Rambling Madison County Spa, Art Center," *Madison County Herald*, 17 January 1963.
38. Quotation from *Along the Gulf.*
39. Ibid.
40. Ibid.
41. Quotation from *Picturesque Vicksburg and the Yazoo Delta* (1895; reprint, Vicksburg, MS: Vicksburg Foundation for Historic Preservation, 1995), 91.
42. Ibid.
43. Ibid.
44. Ibid.
45. Quotation from advertising brochure, "Great Southern Hotel in Gulfport, Mississippi," 1903.
46. Ibid.
47. Quotation from advertising brochure, "Edgewater Gulf, Deep in the Glamorous Old South," n.d.
48. Ibid.
49. Elsie May Chambers, "Dynamite Blasts; Old Hotel Stands," *Jackson Daily News*, 26 July 1971.
50. Quotation from *Sea Coast Echo*, 25 December 1926.

Chapter 3: Churches and Synagogues

1. Christian Schultz, as quoted in James, 242.
2. Lorenzo Dow, as quoted in James, 246.
3. J. B. Cain, as quoted in James J. Pillar, "Religious and Cultural Life 1817–1860," in *A History of Mississippi*, ed. Richard A. McLemore (Jackson: University Press of Mississippi, 1973), 394.
4. Joseph Holt Ingraham, as quoted in Pillar, 385.
5. William Mercer Green, as quoted in Sandra Lee McIntire, "St. John's History Shows Rise, Fall of Plantation Life," *Delta Democrat Times*, 26 October 1992.

6. Mrs. P. E. Metcalfe-Collins, "Sketches of Some of the Pioneers of Washington County," *Papers of the Washington County Historical Society 1910–1915* (reprint, Jackson: Mississippi Department of Archives and History, 1954), 129.

7. William Mercer Green, as quoted in McIntire.

8. Quotation from unnamed source in "Cumberlands Once Prominent Church; Progressed from Log Cabin to Brick," *Oxford Eagle*, 22 August 1957.

9. William Faulkner, as quoted in letter to the editor, *Oxford Eagle*, 13 March 1947.

10. Anne E. Franklin, as quoted in Ken P'Pool, "The Architectural History of a Mississippi Town 1817–1866" (unpublished manuscript, 1990), 32.

11. Julian Street, as quoted in P'Pool, 33.

12. Rowland, *Official and Statistical Register*, 248.

13. Sterling Price, as quoted in Gordon Cotton, "Missouri Father Bannon Was Not a Coward, Nor a Skulker," *Vicksburg Evening Post*, 4 January 1998.

14. Unknown Confederate soldier, as quoted in Cotton, "Missouri."

15. Quotation from 1870 newspaper, as quoted in Gertrude Phillipsborn, "The History of the Jewish Community of Vicksburg, 1820 to 1968" (unpublished manuscript, 1969), 25.

16. Unnamed source, as quoted in Mississippi Department of Archives and History Historic Resources Inventory files on Temple Beth Israel.

17. Clara Lowenburg Moses, as quoted in Wendy Machlovitz, *Clara Lowenburg Moses: Memoir of a Southern Jewish Woman* (Jackson, MS: Museum of the Southern Jewish Experience, 2000), 15.

18. C. P. Miller, as quoted in Tommy Covington, ed., *Heritage of Tippah County, Mississippi* (Humboldt, TN: Rose Publishing Company, 1999), 93–94.

19. Letter from Jefferson Davis, as quoted in "The Church of the Redeemer, Biloxi, Mississippi," *Holland's*, May 1952.

Chapter 4: Public Buildings

1. Gerard Brandon, as quoted in Dunbar Rowland, *Mississippi*, 2 vols. (1907; reprint, Spartanburg, SC: The Reprint Company, 1976), 384.

2. Ibid.

3. Stephen D. Lee, as quoted in John Ray Skates, *Mississippi's Old Capitol: Biography of a Building* (Jackson: Mississippi Department of Archives and History, 1990), 104.

4. Legislative decree, as quoted in William D. McCain, *The Story of Jackson* (Jackson, MS: Hyer Publishing Company, 1953), 49.

5. Joseph Willis, as quoted in McCain, *Story of Jackson*, 52.

6. Commissioners' Report, as quoted in McCain, *Story of Jackson*, 52.

7. Rowland, *Mississippi*, 936.

8. Statement of Saints' Baptist Missionary Association, as quoted in Rhodes, 24.

9. Quotation from January 11, 1923, *Monitor-Herald*, as reprinted in Tommy Hallum, "Courthouses Give Glimpse of Calhoun County's Past," *The Newsletter for the Calhoun County Historical and Genealogical Society Inc.*, 2, no. 1 (1996), 5.

10. Jim Harrelson, as quoted in Hallum, 2–3.

11. Ibid.

12. Quotation from January 4, 1923, *Monitor-Herald*, as reprinted in Hallum, 4.

13. C. D. Ellard, as quoted in Hallum, 4.

14. Legislative decree, as quoted in Anabel Power, "Deaf School Burned Twice," Jackson *Clarion-Ledger*, 6 February 1955.

15. Quotation from unnamed source in "School Now Located on Old Canton Road Was Started in 1954," Jackson *Clarion-Ledger*, 12 May 1954.

16. Epitaph on grave of Robert Hindman in Ripley, Mississippi.

17. William Faulkner, *Requiem for a Nun* (New York: Random House, 1950), 39.

Chapter 5: Industrial Sites

1. A. M. Muckenfuss, "The Development of Manufacturing in Mississippi," *Publications of the Mississippi Historical Society* 10 (1909): 163–80.

2. U. S. Department of Agriculture publication, as quoted in Muckenfuss, 164.

3. Rowland, *Mississippi*, 949.

Bibliography

Along the Gulf. Published by L&N Railroad. 1895. Reprint, Pass Christian Historical Society, 1991.

"B," "Letter from Cooper's Wells." *Hinds County Gazette*, 24 August 1859.

Baldwin, Gloria Butler. "'Mighty Stink' the Smell of History." Jackson *Clarion-Ledger,* n.d.

Barnard, F. A. P. "Autobiographical Sketch of Dr. F. A. P. Barnard." *Publications of the Mississippi Historical Society* 12 (1912): 107–21.

Barner, W. G. "Chickasaw College, Once Essence of Education, Now Nothing But Happy Memories to Graduate." *Tupelo Daily Journal*, 7 May 1953.

Bergeron, Kat. "A Legacy of Buildings." *Biloxi-Gulfport Sun-Herald,* 10 September 1995.

"Great Southern Hotel Name Fitting." *Biloxi-Gulfport Sun-Herald*, 24 March 1985.

"Hotel was Once 'Queen of Coast.'" *Biloxi-Gulfport Sun-Herald,* 26 June 1991.

"Symbol of Survival." *Biloxi Sun-Herald*, n.d.

Bettersworth, J. K. "The Reawakening of Society and Cultural Life, 1865–1890." Chap. 21 in *A History of Mississippi,* edited by Richard A. McLemore. Jackson, MS: University Press of Mississippi, 1973.

Brinson, Carroll. *Jackson: A Special Kind of Place.* Jackson, MS: Hederman Brothers Printing, 1977.

Cabaniss, Frances Allen, and James Allen Cabaniss. "Religion in Antebellum Mississippi." *Journal of Mississippi History* 6, no. 4 (1944): 191–224.

Campbell, Nanci. "Edgewater Hotel Falls." *Biloxi-Gulfport Daily Herald*, 6 August 1971.

Canerdy, Beverly. "134-Year-Old School Fought Fires, Fever." Jackson *Clarion-Ledger,* 15 December 1988.

Carter, Hodding. "A Proud Struggle for Grace: Holly Springs, Mississippi." In *A Vanishing America: The Life and Times of the Small Town*. New York: Holt, Rinehart and Winston, 1964.

Chambers, Elsie May. "Dynamite Blasts; Old Hotel Stands." *Jackson Daily News,* 26 July 1971.

"Valuable Materials Salvaged from Old Deaf School." Jackson *Clarion-Ledger,* 2 December 1951.

City of Hattiesburg. "Historic Hattiesburg: The History and Architecture of Hattiesburg's First Neighborhoods." Manuscript, n.d.

Clark, Christa, and Beth Gallaspy. "Emergency Declared at Fire Scene." *Vicksburg Evening Post*, 15 July 1995.

Clark, Cullen. "First Baptist to Celebrate 91st Anniversary." *Greenwood Commonwealth*, 1 July 1979.

Clinton Parkway Project. "Historic Properties Assessment and Phase II Archaeological Testing." July 1996.

Cotton, Gordon. "Cooper's Well, Once-Famous Resort." *Vicksburg Sunday Post*, 30 June 1974.

"Fire Kindles Interest in Obscure Confederate General." *Vicksburg Evening Post,* 30 July 1995.

Images of America: Vicksburg. Charleston, SC: Arcadia Publishing Co., 1998.

Vicksburg: Town and Country. Charleston, SC: Arcadia Publishing Co., 2001.

"Missouri Father Bannon Was Not a Coward, Nor a Skulker." *Vicksburg Evening Post*, 4 January 1998.

Covington, Tommy, ed. *Heritage of Tippah County, Mississippi.* Humboldt, TN: Rose Publishing Company, 1999.

Crocker, Les. "An Early Iron Foundry in Northern Mississippi." *Journal of Mississippi History* 35, no.1 (1973): 113–26.

"Cumberlands Once Prominent Church; Progressed from Log Cabin to Brick." *Oxford Eagle*, 22 August 1957.

Daigre, Barbara, ed. *The History of Grenada County.* Mission, KS: Intercollegiate Press, 1985.

Davis, William C. *A Way Through the Wilderness.* New York: Harper Collins, 1995.

Dougan, Michael B. "Hermann Hirsch and the Siege of Jackson." *Journal of Mississippi History* 53, no. 1 (1991): 19–33.

Doyle, Don H. *Faulkner's County: The Historical Roots of Yoknapatawpha.* Chapel Hill, NC: University of North Carolina Press, 2001.

Edgewater Gulf, Deep in the Glamorous Old South. Promotional pamphlet. N.p., n.d.

Edwards, Jeff. "Historic Old Hotel Razed, a Victim of Economy." *Jackson Daily News*, 11 June 1982.

Ellis, Dan, and Billy Bourdin. "A Look Back at the Inn-by-the-Sea." *The Progress,* 20 April 1995.

Fairley, Laura Nan, and James T. Dawson. *Paths to the Past: An Overview History of Lauderdale County, Mississippi.* Meridian, MS: Lauderdale County Department of Archives and History, 1988.

Faulkner, William. *Requiem for a Nun.* New York: Random House, 1950.

Gandy, Joan W., and Thomas H. Gandy. *Natchez: City Streets Revisited.* Charleston, SC: Arcadia Publishing Co., 1999.

Natchez: Landmarks, Lifestyles and Leisure. Charleston, SC: Arcadia Publishing Co., 1999.

Gonzalez, John E. "Flush Times, Depression, War and Compromise." Chap. 11 in *A History of Mississippi,* edited by Richard A. McLemore. Jackson, MS: University Press of Mississippi, 1973.

Gordon, James F., Jr. *A History of Belhaven College.* Greenwood, MS: Mississippi Printing Company, 1983.

Gray, Ricky Harold. "Corona Female College (1857–1864)." *Journal of Mississippi History* 42, no. 2 (1980): 129–34.

Great Southern Hotel in Gulfport, Mississippi. Promotional pamphlet, 1903.

Greaves, Linda Thompson et al., eds. *Jackson Landmarks.* Jackson, MS: Junior League of Jackson, 1982.

Gurney, Bill. *Mississippi Courthouses: Then and Now.* Fulton, MS: Itawamba County Times, 1987.

Hallum, Tommy. "Courthouses Give Glimpse of Calhoun County's Past." *The Newsletter for the Calhoun County Historical and Genealogical Society, Inc.* 2, no.1 (1996).

Hamilton, William B. "Jefferson College and Education in Mississippi, 1798–1817." *Journal of Mississippi History* 3, no. 2 (1941): 259–76.

Harrelson, Michael. "Becoming a Village." *Ole Miss Alumni Review* 47 (2000): 30–31, 77.

Haynes, Jane Isbell. *William Faulkner: His Tippah County Heritage.* Columbia, SC: Seejay Society, 1992.

"Heights Academy Closed for Five Years, But 'Prof's' Widow Keeps Up With Boys." *Tupelo Daily Journal,* 5 August 1954.

Hickman, Nollie W. "The Lumber Industry in South Mississippi." *Journal of Mississippi History* 20, no. 4 (1958): 211–23.

Hinds, Thomas S. *William Faulkner and the Tangible Past.* Berkeley: University of California Press, 1996.

Hodge, Jo Dent. "The Lumber Industry in Laurel, Mississippi, at the Turn of the Nineteenth Century." *Journal of Mississippi History* 35, no. 4 (1973): 361–79.

Howell, Elmo. *Mississippi Home Places.* Memphis: n.p., 1988.

Mississippi Scenes. Memphis: n.p., 1992.

Huff, Gordon. "Formal Reception for Stock Holders." *Times Picayune,* 20 December 1926.

Humphrey, George Duke. "Public Education of Whites in Mississippi." *Journal of Mississippi History* 3 (1941): 26–36.

James, D. Clayton. *Antebellum Natchez.* Baton Rouge: Louisiana State University Press, 1968. Reprint, Baton Rouge: Louisiana State University Press, 1993.

Johnson, Collin. "Cooper's Well A Font of Local History." Jackson *Clarion-Ledger*, 19 July 2000.

Johnson, Mrs. Jemmy Grant. "The University War Hospital." *Publications of the Mississippi Historical Society* 12 (1912): 94–106.

Joyce, Dee. "The Great Lady on the Gulf: The History, Restoration and Future of Biloxi's White House Hotel." Manuscript, n.d.

Kimbrough, Julie L. *Images of America: Jackson.* Charleston, SC: Arcadia Publishing Co., 1998.

Lacey, James, Jr. "Blaze Destroys Rambling Madison County Spa, Art Center." *Madison County Herald*, 17 January 1963.

Telephone conversation with author, November 2000.

Ladner, Dawn. "Buena Vista Pioneered Coast Convention and Tourist Business." *Biloxi-Gulfport Sun-Herald*, 18 June 1978.

Longmire, David. "Preservationists Eye Synagogue." *Vicksburg Evening Post*, 4 April 1982.

Lucas, A. K. "Education in Mississippi from Statehood to the Civil War." Chap. 13 in *A History of Mississippi,* edited by Richard A. McLemore. Jackson, MS: University Press of Mississippi, 1973.

Machlovitz, Wendy. *Clara Lowenberg Moses: Memoir of a Southern Jewish Woman*. Jackson, MS: Museum of the Southern Jewish Experience, 2000.

McAlexander, Hubert H. *A Southern Tapestry: Marshall County, Mississippi, 1835–2000.* Virginia Beach, Va.: Donning Company Publishers, 2000.

McCain, William D. "Education in Mississippi in 1860." *Journal of Mississippi History* 22, no.1 (1960): 153–66.

The Story of Jackson. Jackson, MS: Hyer Publishing Company, 1953.

McCarty, Kenneth G., ed. *Hattiesburg: A Pictorial History.* Hattiesburg, MS: Woodland Enterprises, 1989.

McIntire, Sandra Lee. "St. John's History Shows Rise, Fall of Plantation Life." *Delta Democrat Times*, 26 October 1992.

Mead, Carol Lynn. *The Land Between Two Rivers.* Canton, MS: Friends of the Madison County-Canton Public Library, 1987.

Metcalfe-Collins, Mrs. P. E. "Sketches of Some of the Pioneers of Washington County." *Papers of the Washington County Historical Society*, 1910–1915. Reprint, Jackson: Mississippi Department of Archives and History, 1954.

Miller, Mary Warren. E-mail to author, 30 April 2001.

Mississippi: The WPA Guide to the Magnolia State. New York: Viking Press, 1938. Reprint, Jackson, MS: University Press of Mississippi, 1988.

Moore, John Hebron. "Mississippi's Antebellum Textile Industry." *Journal of Mississippi History* 26, no. 2 (1954): 81–98.

Moore, Margaret Deschamps. "Religion in Mississippi in 1860." *Journal of Mississippi History* 22, no. 4 (1960):223–38.

Moreton, Ann. "The Church of the Redeemer, Biloxi, Ms." *Holland's, the Magazine of the South*, May 1952.

Muckenfuss, A. M. "The Development of Manufacturing in Mississippi." *Publications of the Mississippi Historical Society* 10 (1909): 163–80.

Mullen, Bill K. "Historic Wesson Hotel Being Razed." Jackson *Clarion-Ledger,* 11 June 1982.

Olden, Samuel B., Jr. "Hotels, Inns and Taverns in Mississippi, 1830–1860." *Journal of Mississippi History* 5, no. 4 (1943): 171–90.

Oliver, Nola Nance. *The Gulf Coast of Mississippi.* New York: Hastings House, 1941.

Pantenburg, Leon. "State's First Jewish Temple Disappears from Skyline." *Vicksburg Evening Post*, 5 June 1983.

Phillipsborn, Gertrude. "The History of the Jewish Community of Vicksburg, 1820 to 1968." Unpublished manuscript, 1969.

Picturesque Vicksburg and the Yazoo Delta. Vicksburg, MS: Vicksburg Printing and Publishing Company, 1895. Reprint, Vicksburg, MS: Vicksburg Foundation for Historic Preservation, 1995.

Pillar, James J. "Religious and Cultural Life 1817–1860." Chap. 14 in *A History of Mississippi*, edited by Richard A. McLemore. Jackson, MS: University Press of Mississippi, 1973.

Pitts, Stella. "Beth Israel Temple." *Journal of Wilkinson County History* 3 (1992): 265–67.

Powell, Murella. "Inn-by-the-Sea was 'In' Place to Be." *Biloxi-Gulfport Sun-Herald*, 3 October 1996.

Power, Anabel. "Deaf School Burned Twice." Jackson *Clarion-Ledger*, 6 February 1955.

"Pages from an Old Scrap Book." *Jackson Daily News*, 13 March 1949.

P'Pool, Kenneth H. "The Architectural History of a Mississippi Town 1817–1866." Unpublished manuscript, 1990.

Rhodes, Lelia G. *Jackson State University: The First Hundred Years*. Jackson, MS: University Press of Mississippi, 1979.

Roark, Belinda. Telephone conversation with author, November 2000.

Rogers, Ralph J. "The Effort to Industrialize." Chap. 31 in *A History of Mississippi,* edited by Richard A. McLemore. Jackson, MS: University Press of Mississippi, 1973.

Rowland, Dunbar. *Mississippi.* 2 vols. 1907. Reprint, Spartanburg, SC: The Reprint Company, 1976.

The Official and Statistical Register of the State of Mississippi: 1912. Nashville, TN: Brandon Printing Company, 1912.

Sansing, David G. *Making Haste Slowly: The Troubled History of Higher Education in Mississippi.* Jackson, MS: University Press of Mississippi, 1990.

———. *The University of Mississippi: A Sesquicentennial History.* Jackson, MS: University Press of Mississippi, 1999.

Sansing, David G., Sim C. Callon, and Carolyn Vance Smith. *Natchez: An Illustrated History*. Natchez, MS: Plantation Publishing Company, 1992.

Sansing, David G., and Carroll Waller. *A History of the Mississippi Governor's Mansion.* Jackson, MS: University Press of Mississippi, 1977.

Scott, Roy V., and Charles D. Lowery. *Old Main: Images of a Legend.* Harmony House Publishers, 1995.

Skates, John Ray. *Mississippi's Old Capitol: Biography of a Building.* Jackson, MS: Mississippi Department of Archives and History, 1990.

Smith, Suanna. "Washington, Mississippi: Antebellum Elysium." *Journal of Mississippi History* 40, no. 2 (1978): 143–65.

Stockstill, E. H. "A Landmark Burns." *Vicksburg Evening Post*, 14 July 1995.

Stockstill, Eugene. "Biloxi Church Ties Coast's Past to Present." *Biloxi Sun-Herald*, 28 November 1998.

Sullivan, Charles L., and Murella Hebert Powell. *The Mississippi Gulf Coast: Portrait of a People.* Sun Valley, CA: American Historical Press, 1999.

Sumrall, Robbie Neal. *A Light on the Hill: A History of Blue Mountain College.* N.p., 1947.

Taylor, Herman E. *Faulkner's Oxford: Recollections and Reflections.* Nashville, TN: Rutledge Hill Press, 1990.

Taylor, Louise. "Soon, Only Memories Will Remain." *Biloxi-Gulfport Sun-Herald,* 24 November 1993.

Turitz, Leo E., and Evelyn Turitz. *Jews in Early Mississippi.* Jackson, MS: University Press of Mississippi, 1995.

Turner, Cal. "Cooper Well [*sic*] Once Ruled Social Life." Jackson *State-Times*, 11 September 1960.

Walton, Gerald. "Early Campus Buildings." Presentation at University Celebration Weekend, Oxford, Mississippi, 27 May 2001.

Weatherby, Mrs. Robert H. Family history of McCutchen family.

Williams, Rosemary. *Cross City Chronicle.* N.p., n.d.

Williamson, Joel. *William Faulkner and Southern History.* New York: Oxford University Press, 1993.

Wilson, Jack Case. *Faulkners, Fortunes and Flames*. Nashville, TN: Annandale Press, 1984.

Winter, Robert Milton. *Shadow of a Mighty Rock.* Franklin, TN: Providence House Publishers, 1997.

Wiseheart, David. Telephone interview with author, 1 November 2000.

Index